Praise for *I Want to Die but I Want to Eat Tteokbokki*

"A testament to the gradual nature of therapy's cumulative healing effects, *I Want to Die* should resonate with anyone who eagerly transcribes every nugget of advice they get." —*BuzzFeed*

"At once personal and universal, this book is about finding a path to awareness, understanding, and wisdom." —*Kirkus Reviews*

"Earnest . . . clever . . . [Baek Sehee] uses months of (real) transcripts from her therapy sessions to explore her own depression and anxiety, always tiptoeing toward something like self-awareness." —*Chicago Tribune*

"With candor and humor, Baek offers readers and herself resonant moments of empathy." —*Booklist*

"For readers feeling a little icy around the edges, [Sehee's] memoir promises to defrost." —Wired.com

"[*I Want to Die but I Want to Eat Tteokbokki*] is a therapeutic salve . . . Sehee's memoir is a connective tissue for all of us looking for a silver lining." —PopSugar

"This book will comfort anyone who's ever been depressed, anxious, or just frustrated with themselves." —*Real Simple*

"Baek Sehee ingeniously combines elements of memoir and self-help . . . She offers an intimate look into one patient's experience in therapy and her own analysis of and takeaways from those sessions . . . Everyone is just trying to be as okay as possible, after all—and seeing Sehee's processing of that in *I Want to Die but I Want to Eat Tteokbokki* is sure to make readers feel a little less alone in their own attempts." —*Shelf Awareness*

"Sehee is honest and authentic throughout . . . [*I Want to Die but I Want to Eat Tteokbokki*] will resonate with young people who suffer from similar forms of depression and anxiety." —*Library Journal*

Reader Reviews for *I Want to Die but I Want to Eat Tteokbokki*

"This book felt like a hug, like a pat on the back that says 'You're doing fine. You're okay—and even if you're not, you will be, someday.'" @chroniqled

"Like nothing I've ever read . . . the raw honesty and candid writing on mental health is to be commended." @amongthewordflowers

"If there was one word to sum up this book it is: seen." @sazloureads

"While reading, I remember thinking 'so other people live like this too' and sometimes that can be the most comforting thing to realize." @sixofpages_

"An honest and candid account of the ways in which our brains often set out to sabotage but a reminder that self-kindness can go a long way." @meg.in.a.book

"The unique feeling of knowing someone in the world is not ok right now either. And both of you will be fine." @literallysimple

"This read was encouraging and reminded me that progress can be made (albeit slowly, but what healing does not take time?)." @badgalgoodbooks

"When I picked it up, I wanted to love this book, and when I finished reading it, I loved it more than I expected. This book will be on top of my comfort reads now, and I will revisit it very often going forward." @thegeekybookreader

"The transcripts are incredibly honest and offer a brave insight into how the mind can trick you into believing certain situations are far more fearful than they actually are in reality." @anon.reads

"For those of us who can relate to the unassuming persistent, spread-out weight of sadness that doesn't feel quite worthy of the title 'depression', this is THE book." @thenovelconversation

I Want
to Die
but I
still
Want
to Eat
Tteokbokki

I Want to Die but I *still* Want to Eat Tteokbokki

further conversations with my psychiatrist

Baek Sehee

BLOOMSBURY PUBLISHING

NEW YORK · LONDON · OXFORD · NEW DELHI · SYDNEY

BLOOMSBURY PUBLISHING
Bloomsbury Publishing Inc.
1385 Broadway, New York, NY 10018, USA

BLOOMSBURY, BLOOMSBURY PUBLISHING, and the Diana logo
are trademarks of Bloomsbury Publishing Plc

First published in 2024 in Great Britain by Bloomsbury Publishing
First published in the United States 2024

죽고 싶지만 떡볶이는 먹고 싶어 2
I Want to Die but I Still Want to Eat Tteokbokki
By Baek Sehee

Copyright © Baek Sehee, 2019

All Rights Reserved.

Original Korean edition published by HEUN Publishing.
English translation rights arranged with Bloomsbury Publishing
Plc through BC Agency.

English translation © Anton Hur, 2024

This book was published under an agreement with the author's psychiatrist.
Identifying information on the relevant clinic has been withheld by request.
We ask for the reader's understanding on this matter.

ISBN: HB: 978-1-63973-230-2; eBook: 978-1-63973-232-6

Library of Congress Cataloging-in-Publication Data is available.

2 4 6 8 10 9 7 5 3 1

Typeset by Newgen KnowledgeWorks Pvt. Ltd., Chennai, India
Printed and bound in the U.S.A.

To find out more about our authors and books visit www.bloomsbury.com
and sign up for our newsletters.

Bloomsbury books may be purchased for business or promotional use.
For information on bulk purchases please contact Macmillan Corporate
and Premium Sales Department at specialmarkets@macmillan.com.

CONTENTS

A NOTE ON THE CONTENT

For readers who appreciate a warning: this book contains material that some might find disturbing, including accounts of self-harming behavior, disordered eating, and suicidal ideation.

This book is not intended as universal advice nor as a substitute for individualized professional attention but rather as a record of one individual's experience.

TO THE READERS OF THE ENGLISH EDITION

When reading this book, you might feel embarrassment or shame or judgement, as if you're reading an old diary entry of your own. When that happens, close the book for a moment. Remind yourself that this is someone else's story and try to separate it from those feelings. Understanding that we are different, perhaps you'll see points of connection between you and me on these pages that help and console you. That is my hope.

I still return often to these words from an overseas reader, and I wish to repeat them to you. *I love and cherish your story. And I am your friend.*

Baek Sehee

PROLOGUE

CONFRONTING THE WOUNDS I NEVER THOUGHT I HAD

I've thought about self-pity a lot in preparation for this second book. Excessive self-pity often leads to depression for me. There are inner wounds that haven't healed, and my therapy has enabled me to realise, bit by bit, what kind of wounds they are and their reasons for existing.

But to know one's wounds and to pity oneself for them are two different things. Self-pity isn't necessarily bad, but perhaps people think badly of it because those who self-pity tend to concentrate on their own suffering and ignore the pain of others. I was afraid I was such a person or would become such a person.

The more my therapy progressed, and the more my wounds healed and the scars turned faint, the more vulnerable I became to suffering. It was too easy to uncover buried hurts and immerse myself in depressive thoughts again.

Familiarity felt like safety to me. Which is why, whenever depression or emptiness came calling, I was all too eager to open the door of self-pity and go right inside. It was a comfortable room where I had spent a lot of my time before. And despite how easily I could've stepped out of it and moved on with my life, I often locked myself inside. As if this familiar suffering was something I could enjoy to my heart's content before going back to my life.

I no longer consider depression as 'the flu of the mind.' For someone who has lived with depression as long as I have – to the point where it's like your second shadow – the disease is more like an incurable chronic illness than a brief cold. It needs constant management, and while you might get better, it's a lifelong journey. So I've decided to expunge the term 'completely cured' from my mind. I'm not simply accepting that this is the way it is and always will be, though. I am trying to find ways not to resort to familiar self-indulgent tendencies whenever I feel depressed, not to feel sorry for myself because of my wounds, or entering that dark room of self-pity. I want to feel what I am feeling and not measure my pain against the pain of others.

This book will not be a useful guide to those seeking a complete cure for depression. But it will be enough, for me, if showing the deepest inner wounds of an individual helps the reader see into their own darkness within. I have held the hands of many people already – and I am ready to hold the hands of many more.

1

WHAT'S WRONG WITH WANTING TO BE LOVED?

'The "size" of human suffering is absolutely relative.'
—Viktor Frankl, *Man's Search for Meaning*
(trans. Ilse Lasch)

Early one Saturday morning, I picked up a new release by Roxane Gay: one of my favourite authors. It was a book titled *Hunger*, and it was my first time reading her autobiographical essays, which made me open to the first page with a feeling of anticipation. But astonishingly – even to me – I burst into tears at the foreword and spent the rest of the time reading the book in pain, putting it down on occasion to rest, though my tears would not stop flowing. It made me realise I had never been honest with myself, even as I'd baldly declared how revealing my darkness to the light was the way to become free. Every childhood memory where I was lonely and hurt and sad from lack of love (maybe not every memory) rose to the surface, unfurling in vivid scenes in my mind.

My crushes had been constant since middle school, but no one had ever accepted my affections. In my third year when I gripped the sleeve of a boy I liked, teasing him, his friend standing nearby picked up on my interest and mocked his friend, saying 'Baek Sehee must like you!' My crush looked embarrassed. In high school there was someone who treated me like I didn't exist once they realised I had a crush on them. There was also the one who toyed with my emotions, and, inevitably, the ones who liked my friends more than me. There were times when I was loved, of course. But as I read *Hunger*, only the hurt from those times came to mind. Memory is not accurate, and it can be rearranged any way you want: to be more extreme or more stimulating.

But it was as if a few pieces of the larger puzzle – the reason for my passivity in my relationships or the cause of my anxiety over the ones where I'd been the side to initiate – were falling into place. 'The person I like doesn't like me. I wanted to be loved by this person, or maybe I wanted to be loved by everyone, but I will never be loved.' These thoughts kept me in the thrall of self-hate and feelings of unworthiness. And I also questioned whether I could ever truly love someone.

Yesterday, I told my partner all of this at length. I hadn't forced myself to consider why I was telling, and I wouldn't have had a clear answer. Would I get better by saying it out loud? I feared my partner would be disappointed once they learned how worthless, how unloved, and how dismissed I had been in my past.

Psychiatrist: (*A sore throat has made it difficult for them to speak.*)

Me: So, doctor, I've been well, but there was a moment where I crumbled for a bit. Does therapy help me bounce back better from setbacks? Because I think my recovery speed has improved a little. I recently read this book titled *Hunger* by Roxane Gay. It's full of the author's candid thoughts on her body and life. She goes into the darkness a lot, and I started crying right from the foreword. And all these memories, not ones I erased completely but ones I wanted to forget and tear up and suppress, they kind of gushed up inside me. Is that something that can happen?

Psychiatrist: Of course.

Me: It was fascinating. Reading that book made the memories unfurl in my mind's eye in a panorama. I jotted down the memories as they came. And I realised that I haven't been honest with myself. What I mean is, of course we don't need to be completely honest with everyone. But it made me realise, *I haven't been honest with myself, even, I've only been honest with myself insofar as I could stand it.* It was so devastating in that moment that I had this unbearable feeling, you know? (*Rummages, looking for my notes.*) In other words, 'I realised I had never completely accepted myself as I am, that I had never embraced my past and wanted only to rid myself of it, and ended up suppressing it, and now my past self and present self cannot connect or separate properly and are in a kind of limbo.'

Like this, for example: If I'm not going to embrace the past-me, then I should bury her and live my life being satisfied with the present me, but I can't do that, and present-me, which is supposed to be different from and stronger than past-me, ends up being tangled up with past-me, making me think, 'Oh, I'm just the same as the old me. This is just a shell.'

Psychiatrist: Can you tell me more about past-me?

Me: (*Talks about the times I was denied love.*) I thought a lot yesterday about whether I would tell you or my partner first, but seeing how unwell you are now makes me glad I told my partner first (*because the psychiatrist can't speak well today*). If I hadn't let it out yesterday, I would not have been in a good place today. I guess everyone has different ways of healing. I think there's no need for absolute truth all the time. And there's nothing more violent than forcing the truth out of someone, making them confess against their will. But still, I know myself. The path to freedom and relief has always been letting the light in as opposed to burying something or running away from it. No matter how hard it may be. This letting in the light has made me stronger and minimised a lot of things that used to loom large for me. Like growing up in poverty or having eczema.

I think the past that I really wanted to keep hidden just wasn't ready to be revealed yet. That's my interpretation of it, at least. I'd locked it away in my subconscious and pretended the past was past and the old me had nothing to do with me, but that didn't mean I was healed, it had remained a wound this whole time. Maybe, if I were to put a positive spin on it, the memories resurfaced because I am ready to accept them now?

Psychiatrist: Was it difficult bringing it up with your partner? What went through your mind?

Me: I did worry whether they would look down on me. I was nervous about it, but I really wanted to tell them. As I've said in here before, I would rather reveal myself, and if the other person wants to leave me because of that, they can leave. But my partner couldn't understand why I would think they'd look down on me or be disappointed in me. Like they couldn't understand why I'd even think anyone would come to such conclusions. When I told them about my past where I was hated so much, they said they had never in their lives hated someone for being ugly, fat, or having bad skin. That such things were out of one's control (*I wish everyone was like that*). They said this to me as if this should be the norm, that any other attitude would be surprising. It shocked them that my classmates had been disgusted by my skin, that I thought of myself as, maybe not ugly – I don't think I was ugly – but plump, and that's why I thought I was ugly? That I would be ashamed about my crushes being embarrassed about my liking them. I would think, 'I'm someone who inspires disgust, that's the value that I have.' And what's even more disgusting is how I would internalise that gaze and perpetuate it. I would look down on someone who liked me, and out of my obsession with weight, hate people I perceived as fat. My hate was all twisted, but in the end, I think I was projecting myself onto them, seeing myself in them.

Once I said these things, it all felt like it had been nothing. Well, maybe not nothing. But something like, *I guess that wasn't such a big deal.* A kind of lightness, a sense of being someone else, someone who might think, 'Why on earth would you have felt that way?'

Psychiatrist: Because when you're thinking something, your emotions are mixed up in it. And you're still inside your 'feeling at the time.' But once you put the situation outside of yourself by using words, you can judge the situation from an observer's perspective. Rationally.

Me: Right? Before I talked about it, the memories and the shame were all mixed together and felt like a huge deal, but once I'd exorcised it using words, the feelings dissipated, and I was left with mere words. Which made me annoyed, like, 'Wow, all that suffering, once put into words, is just nothing.' They just seemed like the kinds of thoughts anyone might think during their adolescence. Like I was being overdramatic all this time.

Psychiatrist: If you think back between then and now, you simply did not have the capacity to handle the pain then. You basically put it away in a secret box inside you for a bit, waiting for a time when you might be able to face it. You were thinking, 'I'm struggling from day to day, I can't handle any of my wounds right now, and what if I get hurt again?' And rather than face that danger, you put away even the feelings you liked. You put them away so thoroughly, you've become unaware that you put them away at all.

But now your life is completely different, you have someone who loves you by your side, and the people you associate with are different. Your skin condition is better managed now. It was really hard for you when you were younger. But from the perspective of the present, a physical wound merely makes you think, 'It hurt really bad when it happened, but now there isn't even a scar'? Or you might look at a scar and think, with some distance, 'Oh yeah, that used to hurt pretty bad.'

Me: (*Bursts into tears.*) Yes, it really is like that.

Psychiatrist: I'm sorry. About my voice.

Me: Not at all. Honestly, reading that book, it was like that secret box, which was wrapped up tight – the book ripped off the wrapping in one go. Or maybe it was me doing the ripping. I felt a great release. Practice will make perfect, but for now, if someone compliments me, I have the strength to just casually say, 'Thanks. When I was a kid, I wasn't much and no one liked me, but that's whatever.'

Psychiatrist: Yes. And like you said just now, about telling your partner about it, you looked for their reaction. We've come to a place where that's possible, in other words. I think you need to be cognisant that you've come far enough from your past to tell someone about it and be looking for that someone's reaction. The present you is no longer past you.

Me: Yes, I feel much stronger. To be honest, I didn't like that trauma and wounds could connect to the present. I think I was afraid I would never be able to leave the past behind. Which is why slogans like, 'The past is nothing, that's not you' were inspiring to me. But I've experienced it first hand now, that the past can only connect to the present . . .

Psychiatrist: It's a good experience. How did you come about the book? Did someone recommend it to you?

Me: No, I have a habit of looking at new releases. And reading is a hobby. I was scrolling through the new releases page on an online bookstore, and the title *Hunger* caught my eye, as did the description 'confessions on the body and hunger.' And I like autobiographical essays. I read the summary and it sounded heartbreaking and I strongly wanted to read it. But the funny thing is, despite instinctively wanting to read it, I put it in my shopping cart and didn't buy it for days, until I thought, 'Oh what the heck,' and purchased it. It happened to be International Women's Day. I took a photo of the cover and opened it and read the first pages and then . . . I couldn't believe it; I was crying just from reading the foreword.

Psychiatrist: How were you feeling before you read the book?

Me: Just a moment (*takes a look at diary*). A Thursday. I was a bit exhausted.

Psychiatrist: What was the reason?

Me: I was busy, for one thing. Meetings at work, and a meeting for my own book. I couldn't rest in the evening for about three days. On Thursday, there was a training session at work, which meant I was in the office until 7 p.m. And on top of that, I'm a little obsessive when it comes to appearing talented. I don't want to seem like I'm bad at my work. When someone else comes up with a good idea at work, my reaction should be, 'Wow, what a great idea!' not 'Why couldn't I have thought of that idea?' I don't know why I'm like this. In the workshops at work, we basically have day-long meetings, and everyone else comes up with terrific ideas all day. It makes me think, 'Ugh should people like me even write books?' and I feel a wave of private despair. But there's a good thing! I don't feel that way today. It was hard at the time, true. And there was a lot of pressure.

Psychiatrist: Did someone put that pressure on you?

Me: No one, absolutely no one does that. It's so hilarious. If someone *had* put pressure on me, my attitude would at least make a little bit of sense.

Psychiatrist: You're putting pressure on yourself because no one else is.

Me: Right? And I'm all sunk in my own feelings, like, 'They're all thinking about it but just not saying it to me, they're all biding their time and seething inside, it's all going to explode someday.' Whew, what a weird assumption.

Psychiatrist: Do you often suffer privately in your own thoughts?

Me: Yes. I get all stewed up in my own negative emotions and then feel the urge to break away from them. Oh, and you know how I said I wrote down my old memories in a notebook? I was sobbing and not in my right mind when I did it. But apparently, the first thing I wrote was the line, 'I want to be ruined.' I'd written about wanting to be ruined since the beginning of our time together. And when you asked, 'What do you mean by "ruined"?', I would answer, just living any way I want to live. And you asked me if that really was what the word 'ruined' meant. And the me of now thinks the current road to ruin is to quit my office job. It's only been four months since I moved to a different part of the company because I wanted to learn something new, and everyone is so busy and there's so much work to be done, and amidst all that me saying, 'I'm quitting because my mental illness is too serious,' would be, from my perspective, the way to ruin myself. Those are the thoughts in my head.

Psychiatrist: Could it be that by pressuring yourself about all this ruining, you're trying to pre-empt it and stop someone else from pressuring you? That this is your way of processing pressure?

Me: Oh. That's right. It's pressure. I feel too much pressure. We were having our workshop yesterday, and you know I have a big fear of corporate life. There were thirteen people sitting in a conference room having a meeting.

It was a pretty light mood, nowhere near suffocating. It's not like there's anyone in our company being a bully or anything. But there's still a hierarchy. For example, when we're all together, we're led by the vice-director, and we sit down and after a brief pause someone goes, 'Is anyone taking notes of the meeting? Anyone with a laptop?' and it's the most recent hire's job to jump up and bring a laptop. It's that kind of place. But I find that so, so scary and oppressive.

And I'm fine with colleagues who are around my age, but when I'm with people who have power and are part of a clique at work, I feel anxiety and dread. 'This person is going to go around talking behind my back. This person hates me and will harm me.' The anxiety and fear really bear down on me. No one has said an unkind word, but I'm already cut off from everyone and adrift on my own. I felt a lot of mental fatigue from that yesterday.

Psychiatrist: You continue to have this fear of being left behind. But before, you hadn't even dared to put yourself in a situation of pressure, now at least you are in a place where you can hold both thoughts: 'I'd rather leave this place than suffer this pressure' and 'No, I still want to prove I can do it.'

Me: You're right. There's a desire to stick it out and prove myself and the desire to quit everything.

Psychiatrist: Right. But without pressure or anxiety, there's no progress, either. If you react to every criticism with, 'Why is that person bothering me?' and there's no change, then that becomes a different problem. I think you should allow yourself a bit of fear and dread for the sake of your own progress. They say we change as we age. Like someone who was politically progressive when young might have moments of anxiety later in life where they think, 'Have I become another conservative curmudgeon?' and then adjust their behaviour accordingly. Your thoughts and behaviours are used to being ruthlessly binary, but if you allowed yourself a bit of space between your thoughts and actions, or if you could just be a bit more flexible like, 'My behaviour might be like this right now but my thoughts are different at least,' then I think you would feel much more comfortable with yourself.

Me: You've talked about transitional periods before, and I think at the time the concept was very obscure to me. But now I wonder if I really am in a transitional period. I had this feeling for the first time that I was successfully transitioning. I want to believe this feeling.

Psychiatrist: Good job.

Me: My partner saying, 'I've never felt hate towards anyone for being fat or ugly or having bad skin' was a real comfort to me. Because it was exactly the right attitude to have.

Psychiatrist: Everyone has those experiences where they have flashbacks to things they don't want to remember. Like when they felt hate towards things they consciously knew it was wrong to hate. They feel shame and make an effort to do better. They may not have always been victims in the past. But that's how you 'become your own person' with your own thoughts, by trying on different attitudes and rolling with the punches that follow. An extreme experience remembered in a single moment cannot and does not explain someone's whole life.

Me: You're right. You know how I've centred the male gaze for a long time in my life, how I wanted to look good to men? The fact that I had such an inclination is so hateful to me. But my partner disagrees, saying they don't understand why that should be hateful, asking me 'What is hate?' I replied, 'Hate?

Something I really, really dislike? More than dislike,' and they still didn't understand. They said, 'So you feel hatred towards your child self, who was all mired in her own feelings and misunderstandings, and wanted to look good in front of some other silly kid?' And I said no. Because, really, that wasn't the case. I think the younger me was cute. Maybe I feel a bit sorry for her. Which made me think, 'That's right, there's nothing hateful about any of this. It's just what it is. What's wrong with wanting to come off well? What's wrong with wanting to be loved?' This thought reassured me.

And among the blurbs for *Hunger* was one about the difficulty not necessarily of *revealing* one's hurt and suffering but revealing them as clearly as this book does, for self-pity and narcissism are the worst traits in writing, and it would've been so easy to fall into those attitudes. I happen to think I have strong self-pity. This mention of self-pity and narcissism ruining one's writing made me feel hurt. Why are those the worst traits?

Psychiatrist: Well. I don't really know about that. I suppose if one has self-pity and narcissism at the same time, their perspectives would be very narrow. Maybe that everything they think is correct. Or they connect everything to their own issues and wounds.

Me: Do I also have narcissism and self-pity?

Psychiatrist: I don't think your narcissism is that strong. Your self-pity is a bit strong.

Me: Is self-pity so bad?

Psychiatrist: No, why would it be? I haven't read the book but maybe the blurb is criticising the kind of books that are like, 'Have you ever suffered as much as me? I've had the hardest time ever. If you haven't suffered as much as I, you should not even bother to speak.'

Me: Oh ... oh, I see. I get it. Self-pity worries me a lot, I also think my self-pity is very strong. And I get hurt so easily; I have so many memories of getting hurt. But I've probably hurt someone somewhere, too, I'm sure. But I only remember the hurt I received. My writing tends to be a record of the wounds I've sustained, and I censor this through the gaze of others while fearing what others will think: 'What awful self-pity, what pathetic victim cosplay.'

Psychiatrist: We live in a world where we are allowed to express ourselves freely, do we not? And lots of people find comfort in the kind of books that go, 'This was how hard it was for me, and this is how I overcame it.' Isn't it more of a matter of writing simply about the things you've experienced instead of whatever you think would garner the most pity?

Me: Yes, that would be better. Not to be overwhelmingly emotional. And I keep remembering things I had forgotten.

Psychiatrist: That's a good sign. Your suppressed memories are being released. There are things we've hidden so far down in our subconscious that we can't even remember them. But once the floodgates open, they start coming back, and it's like the subconscious has determined that you are now capable of handling the heft of these emotions, that you can at least begin to address them.

Me: I did have the feeling that I've been a lot stronger lately. This new trust in myself is a nice feeling to have.

Psychiatrist: That's good to hear.

Me: I hope you feel better soon. See you next week.

Psychiatrist: Thank you.

WHEN I ABSORB ONLY THE WORDS THAT HURT ME

'I am so sick and tired of being judged for how I look.'

Whenever I try to make myself look better because I fear I look ugly, I end up ruining even the nice parts of my appearance. I am so sick and tired of being judged for how I look. The comparisons to my pretty older sisters were constant when I was little. When we met with our aunts, they would ask our cousins to pick which of my older sisters was prettier. I was not popular throughout school (and nothing has changed since then). My past partner's friends would tell my partner that I was not pretty at all. I've been described as being like a North Korean woman, old-fashioned. Or that I'm not the kind of woman men like. A boy who was working the same part-time job as me said to me one day that if I came to the place he volunteers at, I would be considered a goddess. Even when I *was* complimented for being pretty, there would always be caveats laden with sexual harassment like, 'but you don't have sex appeal.' There were jokes about how I should get that surgical procedure that makes you taller. When I went to interview for part-time jobs, I'd be told my application photo looked very different from the real me. I've heard so many times that I'm deceptively photogenic, even though I don't bother with airbrushing anymore. There were people who would chime in to say, 'But Sehee's not pretty,' when I was being praised in front of other people. I only feel a tinge of bitterness when I meet someone who says my face is the most beautiful in the world. I hate the way my face looks, so who cares how many times a day someone says I'm pretty? I will only continue to absorb the words that are critical of me.

2

THINNESS: THE PRESSURE I CAN'T ESCAPE

When I was little, I wasn't interested in my body. The only thing about it that really concerned me was the eczema, but it was rare that anyone commented on my figure. All I remember was that my body was considered unremarkable. But I loved to eat, and because I grew in height throughout my elementary and early middle-school years, I could maintain a standard weight without dieting.

But one day during the winter break of my third year in middle school, I was wearing a sleeveless shirt while watching television when my older sister chastised me. 'Hey, what's up with your arms? Why are you so fat? What happened to you?' Around that time, someone posted on an anonymous online message board that I looked fat. For the first time, I began to worry that I had a weight problem and began comparing my body to those of other girls and women. Hate crept into my feelings about my body. 'I have fat on my belly, but this girl doesn't. I have thick arms, but that girl has thin arms.' The flesh on my belly, face, and arms became objects of disgust for me.

Only having thought of women's bodies as being 'fat' or 'thin' before, my categories became more detailed. Now there was 'skinny,' 'just skinny enough,' 'standard,' 'slightly plump,' and other descriptors of that nature. I thought everyone would look down on me if I gained weight, and this was true to a degree. This pressure to lose weight that began in high school continued into adulthood after I achieved my goal weight, and I still struggle with it today.

Me: How are you today? Does your throat still ache?

Psychiatrist: It's much better. And how have you been?

Me: Me? I've been all right, but my dieting has made me a mess . . .

Psychiatrist: What kind of mess?

Me: At our company, we're putting together something called a psychology diary. It's a collection of entries on the kinds of psychological concerns women in their twenties and thirties might have, like the pressure to lose weight, addiction to relationships, compulsive spending, and anger management. I was searching for an author for the dieting part so I looked at a lot of books. There were tests about eating disorders in them, and they said you have an eating disorder if you score above twenty-seven. I scored forty-six. Which made me think, 'Do I have a disease?' I wasn't caught up in this thought necessarily, but let's say I became more cognisant of it. A work colleague of mine did it, and she only got an eight. It made me feel like I was ruled by my appetite, by my relationship to food.

I've put on so much weight that the clothes I wore in the summer don't fit me anymore.

The trousers I wore with a belt in the summer fit perfectly now. That was so annoying it drove me up the wall.

I think I'm a lot better now psychologically. I feel depressed a lot less, and I guess I'm also too busy to feel that way these days. But the pressure to diet is still there.

Psychiatrist: Aside from when you put on clothes, how do you feel when you see your body?

Me: I hate looking at my body. Because I hate it so much. I get stressed.

Psychiatrist: You disgust yourself?

Me: Yes, I feel plump. Maybe I'm not fat, but plump?

Psychiatrist: Does that immediately affect your eating?

Me: The stress makes me eat more, if anything. Like I decided to give up. I can't control my appetite, I don't eat regularly, and I'm stressed out over eating. The only meal I enjoy is my first meal of the day, but by the second meal I eat under a lot of stress. Wouldn't it be better if I just enjoyed eating, since I'm eating anyway? It's the same pattern every time. And just because I have a good lunch, it doesn't mean I'm not hungry at dinner, either. So

I starve myself during lunch. But I heard that the more you starve, the more you crave sweet things.

Psychiatrist: That's true. Because your gut-brain axis gets thrown out of joint.

Me: Yes. I keep thinking I need to change. If I skip a meal one day, I find myself bingeing on crisps the next. I ate three whole bags of them in one go recently. It makes my insides churn and I get thirsty and scratchy all over and my body feels awful. And I regret it, which makes my mind feel awful.

Psychiatrist: You're not a big veggies eater?

Me: I might have an apple at lunch. Or a salad.

Psychiatrist: If you feel hungry all the time, you're bound to feel the urge to be compensated for such sacrifices as well. You have to find a way to stop the cycle.

Me: You're right. Skipping meals is one thing, but once I start eating, I can't stop putting food in my mouth.

Psychiatrist: That happens to me sometimes, too.

Me: Really? In the mornings, my medications are great for controlling my appetite. I don't binge junk food at nights like I used to. Those three bags of crisps were ones I bought on my way to work and ate over the morning. To the point where people were asking me if I was stressed about something. My partner seemed really worried seeing me like this and told me I should try to discuss it with you, if it's something that can be controlled with medication. Saying that my biggest obsession these days was my weight, that I didn't seem to be able to control it on my own, that I should talk it over with you.

Psychiatrist: The ironic thing here is that from an objective perspective, you aren't anywhere near obese or fat. Your desire to lose weight is purely for your own satisfaction. You have a normal weight. Sure, there are people who take medication to suppress their appetites, with some success. It can be one way of handling it. But it's better to find ways in your daily life to substitute certain behaviours. Crisps for example. Just going, 'I am quitting crisps from this moment on,' does not make it any easier to carry out. You need to replace the habit with something. Quitting something cold turkey can immediately create a deprivation in your life.

Me: There's nothing that can be done with medication?

Psychiatrist: Would you like to take an appetite suppressant? I don't find it very effective so I take it on and off, but it can be very different for others.

Me: I'd like to try that.

Psychiatrist: It's not the same as the appetite suppressants that were popular in the past. Diet clinics used to prescribe one which would have a strong effect in the beginning that wouldn't last long, then yo-yoing would follow. The more recent medication is less effective in the beginning, they say, but it is proven to be more effective in the long run. Do you take vitamins? You should take vitamin C every day. People on diets in particular don't absorb nutrients so well. I think you should at least take vitamin pills.

Me: All right.

Psychiatrist: A Korean family medicine research department once did a comparative study of people who take vitamin C and those who don't and concluded that those who do end up with better results. At the very least, they have antioxidant properties, which to some extent mitigates the cellular ageing that comes with dieting.

Me: That's good to know. Because I'm definitely ageing.

Psychiatrist: You're ageing?

Me: Of course. I don't pay much attention to my health. My partner pays so much attention to their health. They're afraid of ending up with costly health problems later down the road, dying in pain, and getting sick in general. But I take health for granted. Oh wait, I wanted to ask you this. I think I tend to obsess over things other people don't think are very important, and neglect things that others feel are very important. For example, I'm resigned to getting glaucoma and not being able to see, but I react incredibly sensitively to the hurtful things people say and keep that hurt alive in me for a long time.

Psychiatrist: That's not simply a matter of importance, but about what meaning something has to you personally. For example, if you think you'll just go to the hospital if for whatever reason you get sick, then you won't necessarily feel anxious about getting sick in the future.

Me: Oh, it's a difference in perspective?

Psychiatrist: Yes. Someone else could look at what you think is a big deal from the outside and think, 'Why is she so caught up in that tiny thing?' Everyone has a different sense of what's important.

Me: Does my lack of concern for my health and disregard for physical pain have anything to do with my psychology?

Psychiatrist: From one perspective, it might have something to do with a desire to punish oneself. A desire to prevent oneself from becoming too happy.

Me: I see. I do feel like things are improving these days.

Psychiatrist: Exactly, such as how you're taking control of this trousers situation, choosing to think, 'I'd rather not obsess over my weight anymore!' You have control over more areas of your life.

Me: And before, when I didn't have any confidence in myself, I would be so affected by what people said about me, their judgements and advice. But that happens less often now. Like, my choices? I put more emphasis on those, and I don't feel as influenced as I used to. That kind of thing.

Psychiatrist: Can you ignore outside voices altogether?

Me: Yes. 'I'm much happier and things are getting better, why should I think otherwise? Why am I wrapped up in silly worries?' I'm able to think that way now. In the past, I might think, 'I must be doing something really wrong, I must look really weird right now.' Or 'What if I'm not getting better and I'm really getting worse but I'm the only one who doesn't realise it?' Those anxieties used to be really strong, but these days, I don't think that way so much. My older sister used to worry aloud about me a lot. I no longer feel affected by that.

Psychiatrist: Then do you occasionally feel disgruntled when someone voices worries about you? Like, 'Why doesn't that person mind their own business?'

Me: I do think, 'They should back off and take care of themself first.'

Psychiatrist: Good. Your life comes first. We live in a world where there are all kinds of different lifestyles, and when you see others living their lives you might think, 'I suppose that's another way of living,' but when it comes to yourself you tend to take someone else's perspective, the worst perspective possible, when there's no reason to take such a narrow view of your own self and feel hurt about it. Like tattoos.

There are people who might think, 'What if they regret that later in life?' and still others who go, 'Wow, that's really cool!' Just like the time you got a tattoo, you must let go of your narrower thoughts and think, 'I have a reason for doing this, I'm doing it because I like the way it looks.' Keep thinking of your life that way.

Me: You're right. Honestly, I've improved a lot lately. But there's one anxiety I still have: that I won't measure up at work, that I'll be thrown aside, looked down upon, humiliated.

Psychiatrist: You might never be free from that. We're all affected by others to some degree and we can't control everything about our lives. For example, let's say you're headhunted by another company. You might feel good about that at first, but an ordeal awaits you where you've got to adjust to a new workplace. That's pressure. Everyone has stress and pressure like that to some degree.

Me: Do you have pressures?

Psychiatrist: Of course. There might be a patient who I thought was getting better, but when they don't show up I think, 'Did I do something wrong?'

Me: I see, so there's . . . there's nothing we can really do about that. I think about how much happier I am these days aside from my weight, and how I am going to keep being happy. You know how my book got me some money? I gave some to my sisters and my parents. I haven't made a huge amount of money, but now that I have it, I keep thinking about how I could maintain this much of a financial cushion.

And at work, I receive more stress from my interpersonal relationships than the work itself. It's not like anyone bullies me or even pays me much attention, but I get so stewed up in my own thoughts that it stresses me out. I'm fine with getting stressed about the work, but the people stress? The competitiveness? How you have to keep changing and you must not be left behind? I keep thinking I want to be free from those things.

Psychiatrist: I think you must learn to accept that everyone has such stresses, that no matter how much you're enjoying your job, you will never be completely free from these things. That stress is inevitable. Even in your happiest moment, you can't like absolutely everything about everything. It's just that you happen to be feeling sturdy now, and a little knock here and there isn't going to be enough to topple you, whereas before the smallest knock would've left a painful wound. Telling yourself something like, 'What can I do to hurt less and minimise the suffering, surely I'm not the only one who's hurting right now' can help you along.

Me: Accept it . . . I do feel stress about work, but I really like it, too. Even if I'm really anxious and unsure of my abilities and everyone else seems like a genius, I like the work a lot, despite the stress. Even when it gets to be a lot sometimes. Which is why I used up three vacation days for the week after next. I'm going to Jeju Island for four nights. I told them I would go in lieu of my summer vacation. That I was going to rest a bit and come back refreshed for work.

Psychiatrist: Cherry blossom season. You said just now that everything was fine except your weight. Then I think you should seek change in a different aspect of your life. Like doing an activity for your dates instead of just going to a restaurant together.

Me: My partner asked me to go hiking with them and I said I didn't want to. Usually they let it go at that, but today they kept insisting, 'Come with me, the weather is so nice!', so I went. And once I was there, it was great.

Psychiatrist: But do bear in mind that when trying to lose weight, it's almost impossible to do so by just increasing the amount you exercise . . .

Me: Yes. It's more about what you eat . . .

Psychiatrist: Exactly. And exercise increases your appetite, and you have to eat more if you exercise more. You might consider how you can decrease carbohydrates and sugars in your diet. The thing about sugars is that they satisfy your reward compulsions too simply. Like narcotics, they're instantly rewarding and bring about strong dependencies. If they're strong enough for you to feel the effects as soon as you take them, they become ineffective just as quickly. Sugars are even worse that way.

Let's hold off on the appetite suppressants. Let's talk about the timing of your pills.

Me: I take my pills at about 8.30 in the morning. The ones you gave me for night-times are good. I do still keep waking up in the middle of the night, but I think I feel more rested in the morning?

Psychiatrist: Then let's have you take those at lunch instead of at night.

Me: All right. See you next week.

IT'S JUST AN ORDINARY BODY

'Such a flimsy and strange sliver of power.'

Everyone I know says I've gained weight, which makes me hate going out and meeting people. Hearing that I've gained weight makes me think I've become ugly, that I look heartier makes me think I'm plump. And to me, being plump or fat means being ugly, insignificant, worthless. The gaze of others becomes the gaze I see myself through, piercing into me more sharply than ever. Anxiety over my looks, dieting, mental health, it all presses in around me and manifests in binge eating. I was plump throughout high school and lost weight in college, but that didn't make me pretty. All it did was prevent people from insulting me for walking down the street eating fries, and stopped my family saying things like, 'That's why you're fat' if I have a chocolate after dinner. I liked how people responded with, 'What's there to lose?', when I lamented about wanting to lose weight. Such a flimsy and strange sliver of power. Enough to intoxicate me, make me lose weight for the sake of other people's gaze instead of my own health. These thoughts make the hunger surge in me and I end up losing control again. Everything, as always, is my fault.

3

SEEING MYSELF THROUGH THE EYES OF OTHERS

In my thirty years on earth, the fact of life that has left the biggest impression on me is that other people are really not that interested in what I do. And that makes me sad. Because I am very interested in others. Even if what I'm really interested in is how I look to others (excess of self-consciousness). Still, I'm genuinely interested in others. Where they've been, what thoughts they're having, how they're feeling: I'm curious about all of it. When someone wears something pretty that day, I want to compliment them. I can tell right away if someone has changed their hairstyle or make-up. As good as I am at finding people's flaws, I'm also good at finding their strong points. That's why when I discover someone is not interested in me, I become lonely. When I slip out at lunch to change because I don't like the clothes I had on in the morning but no one notices (as if they should notice such things), or when I realise, after worrying about people staring at me when I have a new haircut, that no one is even looking at me, I feel relief and yet very lonely at the same time.

Me: Hello.

Psychiatrist: How is your appetite? Did it go down a bit?

Me: Uh . . . yes. I think it went down.

Psychiatrist: Did you eat less when your appetite decreased?

Me: Aside from bingeing on biscuits this one time from stress, I think I ate well. Just enough.

Psychiatrist: Why were you stressed that one time?

Me: The thing is . . . this is really bad, but I want to quit my job.

Psychiatrist: Why?

Me: I told my company I had signed a contract to publish my book and they said I wasn't allowed to do that. The CEO said it was something they couldn't understand at all, that it would only hinder my performance at work. I had a long discussion with him, but I came out of it feeling horrible. The company isn't paying me for twenty-four hours of my day; I couldn't understand why they would concern themselves with my personal creative endeavours outside of work. I guess you could say I've gone off the company a bit? I just got completely sick of it. So I'm thinking of saying they have no right to interfere with my hours outside of work like that and if they still won't capitulate, I'm quitting.

Psychiatrist: Have you thought about the repercussions of quitting because of this?

Me: I know I should think about the consequences, but I don't know. I didn't go in on Friday either, because I was sick. I kept thinking that no matter what the consequences, I just wanted to quit. And I hated bowing down and hiding my true feelings because I was afraid people would insult me or hate me. That kept nagging me, which was so incredibly irritating, and which led me to think 'I should quit.'

Psychiatrist: But your feelings, again, have gone right down the path to the extreme option of quitting. This could be quite self-destructive. I understand you feel resentful and angry, but that anger has connected too readily with the prospect of quitting. You're weighing only two extreme choices, like quitting your company or not, or publishing your book or not, in black-and-white thinking.

Me: The other thing is, it's only been four months since I changed divisions, but I've already lost all motivation. The proposals and ideas I've put forth all have not come through, and I'm stuck with whatever book they assign me to. Everyone else seems really busy – I'm the only one who's not. And I don't know what to do about it. It's so, uh, tedious? Unmotivating. Enervating? All of those things . . . again.

Psychiatrist: When you're this disappointed, your perspective naturally skews negative. I think your current state is one of selective attention to the negatives rather than the positives. And the more you think this way, the more you will continue to think this way into the future. I wonder if you should try to understand the situations of others in order to get a little more objective.

Me: How do I understand that?

Psychiatrist: I'm not sure. It depends on the situation in your company . . . there must be a way? But if you don't look around you a bit more and find things out before you decide, this could lead to a situation of self-sacrifice.

Me: Sacrifice? But I don't think of leaving the company as a sacrifice.

Psychiatrist: Wasn't it your original intention to keep working there? I'm only suggesting you saying you're quitting because the work is tedious and you're unmotivated might be you trying to rationalise your current choice.

Me: You mean, I'm letting my emotions get the better of me?

Psychiatrist: It looks like that a little.

Me: But this happened last week and three whole days have passed – my feelings are the same.

Psychiatrist: Because anger is that kind of emotion . . .

Me: Why do I keep feeling this resentment towards them?

Psychiatrist: Anyone would be angry in such a situation. It's your choices here that would differ, depending on your priorities. Everyone responds differently.

Me: I don't know why the prospect of people insulting me makes me feel so fearful. Why should I care so much about that anyway?

Psychiatrist: Well, you dismiss it with 'Why should I care so much about that,' but at the same time, I think you keep internalising the gazes of others and judging yourself through them. Even the emotions you are feeling don't go through any kind of filter before immediately being subjected to this gaze. Which makes you give up on things because of the influence of others, despite such things having value to you or potential for profit. It would be fine in such situations to be a bit more selfish, do things your way, choose the things you feel are more important.

Me: It's not like anyone has insulted me or said anything to me at work, but I keep thinking, 'Someone is going to insult me here, someone really hates me.' I exhaust myself with this anxiety.

Psychiatrist: If someone who has nothing to do with me insults me and I don't hear it myself, who cares? Whether they make fun of you behind your back or not, it has nothing to do with you really. But if someone you really liked hated you, that would be a big hurt. I'm saying you need to distinguish between these two things. You want to be more honest about your own feelings, and try to centre your own thoughts about yourself, pay attention to them over the opinions of others, but you keep putting their perspectives on the same level as your own. Different people will perceive you differently, but if you go down the slippery slope of catering to each of them, the energy you have to spend on those you actually care about will be depleted, and those who are close to you will resent you for it. Which makes you then regret how you haven't been able to be there for the people you love. Doing it the more selfish way, of dividing your relationships into those you care about and those you don't care too much about, will not really create any big problems in the long run. Because that's what everyone does in the end. How about trying to save up as much of yourself as you can, to daringly make the choices that profit you as much as possible and lose as little for you as possible?

And with any choice you make, the question 'Should I or should I not?' is the last decision one makes in the decision-making process. But going directly to this choice means giving up any kind of negotiation or compromise along the way. There is so much for you to gain from those deliberations, but instead the process is reduced to you thinking, 'Screw this, just take it all from me.' And when that becomes a habit, you'll find yourself having lost far more than you anticipated, being left further behind. And that will make you feel even more anxious. I understand your anger and disappointment. But I hope you don't let rage lead you to sabotaging yourself.

Me: By throwing things away all the time?

Psychiatrist: Yes.

Me: You're right. All I feel right now is that this is all just completely disgusting and I want to quit everything.

Psychiatrist: When carrying resentment in your heart and acting on it, you might end up in a regretful situation. Even if you do end up quitting, stay put for now and get everything in order first, and then think about how you can strategise better.

Me: I hate going into work.

Psychiatrist: If you hate it, then it's a good idea to plan out your next move. I want you to believe in the power of rationality.

Me: When my thoughts get into such an extreme dimension, I do think to myself, 'Why on earth do I go on living like this?' There are happy things, but I have to keep competing and coming up with ideas and those anxieties are still larger than the happy things, you know? When my feelings are consumed by rage, I just want to die. I look at my colleagues and they all seem like workaholics to me. They're always working overtime . . . I don't work overtime, and it's just me. I'm the only one who leaves on the dot, who uses up her vacation days, and who takes sick days off, which makes me think the others don't like me at all for it. But I don't want to work too hard at an office.

Psychiatrist: You're trying to slip into the mind of someone else and attempting to figure out what they're thinking or how they would feel and then speaking about them as if they were real thoughts and feelings. This makes you feel guilty, and the guilt manifests in rage sometimes. Anyone who really thinks they're beautiful wouldn't feel affected by a criticism to their looks. But if you say something like, 'I'm insecure about such-and-such,' someone making a joke about what you just said would actually feel traumatic.

Me: (*Not quite understanding.*) What should I do then?

Psychiatrist: Maybe you are being too sensitive and imaginative about these supposed signals your company is sending to you. There's no reason for you to do overtime on work that doesn't require overtime just because everyone else is doing it, for example. But you're perhaps taking it to an extreme level by thinking 'Everyone else is working overtime so I should too' when finishing work on time and enjoying your evening is more important to you.

Me: All right. I just don't understand why the other people work so hard.

Psychiatrist: They have their own reasons, surely.

Me: Which is why I feel so guilty. I feel like I'm the only lazy person there . . .

Psychiatrist: The guilt you're describing isn't from your perspective but from your company's perspective. 'You're not working hard enough if you've had time to write a whole book and publish it with another company.' That's your company's perspective, it shouldn't be yours.

Me: Then how should I be thinking?

Psychiatrist: Your more selfish desires, your personal standards: those are what you need to prioritise here. Think about whether you tend to consider the perspectives and opinions of others as some kind of standard at the expense of your own feelings, branding the latter as wrong. Do you talk about this with your partner as well?

Me: When I say I want to quit they tell me to just quit.

Psychiatrist: What regrets do you think you'll have if you quit?

Me: Regrets? Just the fact that I hadn't worked enough years there for it to matter on my CV, and the money?

Psychiatrist: Those two should be the biggest factors. You say that the others are busy and seem to be addicted to work, which could be a negative in some ways but also positive in others. You said you've been at this new position for only four months, which means the amount of work that has accumulated for the others is probably more than what you have now. This job, remember, is the job you dreamed about having. But if you leave now without having experienced it in full because of random factors, then you may regret it.

Me: I think my head will be clearer when I get back from my trip.

Psychiatrist: What are you going to do until your trip?

Me: I was going to tell them I'm quitting on Monday, but I'm going to wait now.

Psychiatrist: Did you tell your company before you signed your book contract? When were you planning to sign?

Me: Next Wednesday. You should prescribe me two weeks' worth of pills. Because of my trip.

Psychiatrist: I will. And I hope you look at all sorts of different possibilities. Make a list of the advantages you have too.

Me: I'll do that.

Psychiatrist: On your trip, I don't think you should make plans to think about anything – just make sure you relax. I hope you can ease some of the burdens in your heart there.

Me: All right, thank you.

Psychiatrist: Have a good trip.

I DON'T WANT TO BE LEFT OUT, BUT I WANT TO BREAK FREE

'I kept flitting back and forth between emptiness and gratitude.'

We were having an editorial meeting in the afternoon when two of the three items I proposed for the agenda weren't even mentioned. Of course, it could've been that we lacked time, but I didn't feel good about it. I felt like I'd become a useless person. I felt like I was about to fall apart with the knock of a feather: how was I still working at this office? Even I could barely stand someone as fragile and weak as me. Why can't I be a little tougher, a little more resilient, someone who can roll with the punches a little? Instead of making a mountain out of a molehill every time, agonising by myself and wallowing in my hurt.

But the thing is: I really don't want to be an incompetent person. I'm afraid of that. And I'm a coward in the face of competition, which is something that lurks everywhere. In the middle of the editorial meeting, I suddenly had a thought that I was simply going to keep ageing like this, keep competing in meetings like this, and the prospect was too horrendous to contemplate.

49

But because I am a weird person who suffers whether she is happy or unhappy, I think I can chalk it up as an improvement that lately I've been having flashes of gratitude even in the worst moments. I keep flitting back and forth between emptiness and gratitude. Rage and gratitude, the desire to be part of a group and to be free, I've got to accept it, these contradictions. I have to console myself that these contradictory impulses can coexist.

4

I NEEDED A WOUND I COULD SEE

On Sunday, I had a depressive episode. I was all prepared to go to Yeonnamdong, but I ended up lying on my bed again. I filled up on biscuits and beer. Lethargy overtook me and my blanket was as heavy as the lid of a coffin. I wanted to die. When I opened my eyes, it was a little after eight. I drank makgeolli. I read a book, fiddled with my phone and ate chocolates and oranges until I finished the makgeolli. The desire to self-harm hit me like a wave. I wanted to leave a wound on my body that I could see with my own eyes. I lay down to sleep after imagining it for a long time, when an overwhelming urge to cut myself made me get up and take out a knife. I made quite a few cuts, and when I thought that was about enough, I put on my jacket and ran up the four floors to the roof. From there, I looked down at the pavement below. I wasn't afraid of the height, but I was scared of the pain if I fell. I was staring down like that when it occurred to me that if I were drunk enough, I could very well fall off the roof by accident. After a long time, I went back downstairs.

I lay down next to my partner and was staring at my arm when they suddenly woke up from sleep. 'What's wrong with your arm? Did you have an accident?' I fled under the covers in fear. When I mumbled, 'I did it to myself,' my partner stared at me speechless for a long time before getting up and finding ointment to put on my arm. I endured the dawn like that before falling asleep. Stress and anxiety kept following me, and the alcohol gave me a headache and nausea. I broke out in hives. The sunlight shining on my skin in the morning was so repulsive that I drew down the blinds in the room. I read a book for a while before calling my psychiatrist and having a talk. They recommended I check myself in. Tears poured, and my partner and I cried for a long time. I could not understand how things had gotten so bad. I lay in bed for a while longer, took a shower and made my way to the hospital.

Me: Hello (*I am already crying*).

Psychiatrist: You're not at work?

Me: I haven't been back since. I don't ever want to go back.

Psychiatrist: If you become an inpatient, will that be enough grounds for sick leave?

Me: I want to quit, so I'm going to.

Psychiatrist: You can always quit later – I think you should try using your sick days first if you have any. You're not in your normal state right now. Even if we could get you back to your baseline, I think you'd still be in danger of more harm.

Me: I don't want to go to work . . .

Psychiatrist: I know you don't want to. I think at this point you should try to completely forget about work, but this obsession with quitting work is the opposite of trying to forget it.

Me: I want to quit (*repeated ad nauseam*).

Psychiatrist: I'm asking you to decide that later. If you say you want to do it later, no one will stop you. But if you're making this decision when your body and mind are not in the right place, then despite all the thinking you did on the matter, it's difficult to see it as the right choice (*because I do not seem to be in my normal state*). Can you show me the wound?

Me: (*Shows them*).

Psychiatrist: You made more than one cut?

Me: Yes.

Psychiatrist: What did you use?

Me: A knife.

Psychiatrist: How did you feel when you did it?

Me: That it wasn't that bad.

Psychiatrist: And how was it when you saw blood?

Me: Just, 'Look, it's bleeding.'

Psychiatrist: What about relief?

Me: A little bit . . . there was relief.

Psychiatrist: How did you come to start doing it?

Me: I . . . I don't know.

Psychiatrist: Is that whole time a bit hazy now?

Me: Yes. I don't think my feelings or thoughts interfered much with it.

Psychiatrist: Was there some time where you hesitated beforehand?

Me: There was a bit of hesitation.

Psychiatrist: For how long? A day? Since the day before?

Me: No. Like I said the other day, I've always had the urge, and yesterday I was in such a bad state that I was just sitting there all day, you know? And I had a lot to drink. I'd laid down to go to sleep, but I wanted to drink again so I had another whole bottle of makgeolli. And then I thought I should really go to sleep, and lying there I had a strong urge to slit my wrists, and that's when I jumped out of bed and did it.

Psychiatrist: And you remember all that?

Me: I remember the situation but not the thoughts I had inside. I didn't have many thoughts, just . . . 'Oh, I actually did something this time.' I've always had suicidal thoughts. Like falling from a great height? I went up to the roof not because I wanted to fall but because I thought actually looking down from that height would bring me back to my senses. It's a low apartment building, but even from the roof above the fourth-floor level, looking down made me feel scared. It made me think I should fall from an even greater height. I was scared and also kind of not scared. It occurred to me that if I really wanted to, I could get even more drunk and really fall.

Psychiatrist: Did you think of your partner?

Me: I had no intention of falling from there. Because that would harm my partner and my neighbours.

Psychiatrist: You had that thought in that moment?

Me: Not necessarily in that moment; it's a thought I have all the time. Which is why I sometimes look for places like abandoned construction sites.

Psychiatrist: How did you feel when you saw the wounds on your arm?

Me: That I was so . . . pathetic. Petty. Too weak.

Psychiatrist: Didn't the wounds hurt?

Me: I mean, these are very superficial cuts. They're not that deep, which is why they don't ache all that much.

Psychiatrist: As you cut yourself, did you wonder if you might go all the way?

Me: I did think I shouldn't die because of this. Just that this was a way of hurting myself. That feeling . . . there was a freeing sensation from having cut myself, but I didn't like the feeling of cutting my own skin.

Psychiatrist: You said just now that if you got drunk enough, you might do it.

Me: I might, if I got drunk enough.

Psychiatrist: Cutting is up to you, as is going up to the roof, but there are lots of occasions where mistakes can creep in. Like losing your footing when you only wanted a peek over the edge. Or trying on a noose and ending up dead because there was no one nearby to assist you. What do you think it would be like if that happened?

Me: If I died when I wasn't ready to die yet? Well . . . I don't know. If I ended up with a noose around my neck, I think I would struggle to get it off?

Psychiatrist: Yes. But the more you struggle, the more the noose tightens. Generally.

Me: (*Surprised*) Really? But if it's a matter of me losing my footing and falling, I don't think I would have time to think of anything in particular.

Psychiatrist: In any case, I understand to a degree you felt satisfaction from self-harm, but I want you to consider how tragic it would be if there was an accident in the process of seeking that satisfaction. If you weren't really ready to go yet but died anyway or ended up suffering even more after you survived. There are many things in life that aren't going your way right now. When that piles up, there's a tendency to seek out things that you can control, like quitting work or self-harm.

Me: I want to do as I want to. I wondered how much I would have to cut myself to seem like a crazy person.

Psychiatrist: What would it mean if you could seem like a 'crazy person'? Whether that's positive or negative.

Me: That the company people and those around me wouldn't think I was being overdramatic, because they don't really see what I'm going through every day . . . I think I'm being overdramatic a lot actually. But I think they'll finally understand. I thought, when I told them I was quitting, that I could really show them.

Psychiatrist: But what I'm asking is: what's the point of really showing them that?

Me: If I show them, then they'll really understand and think, 'She really isn't in her right mind.'

Psychiatrist: Why do they need to understand that?

Me: I want them to understand.

Psychiatrist: Everyone has their reasons for quitting, I suppose. One finds a better way to make a living or hates one's boss. You felt the need to go through the trouble of disproving their suspicions of your mental state by showing them your body to say: 'I couldn't put into words all the hurt I'm feeling: here's some physical evidence'?

Me: I don't know. I...I just think I'm so ridiculous. Even I (*sigh*) think I'm being too much.

Psychiatrist: You mean you're looking for ways to justify or rationalise being too much or overdramatic? But everyone complains when they're suffering.

Me: Am I just desperate for attention? I just want someone to know how hard it is for me.

Psychiatrist: I think you need to know for yourself how hard it is for you.

Me: But I'm suspicious of that. I go back and forth with it. When it's hard, I think it's really hard. And at the same time, I think to myself, 'What's the big deal with you?'

Psychiatrist: It's because you're influenced by those around you too much. Whether you take a leave of absence or quit, that should be the end of the matter, but then you insist on explaining yourself to other people. And I don't think it's just to other people. I think you're trying to explain it to yourself.

Me: (*Bursts into tears.*) I don't know why I'm like this.

Psychiatrist: I've known someone who cut his own arm. A man, in the military. He did exactly what you did. Cut lines on his forearm and wrist. At first he did a couple and thought, 'People are going to think I'm just doing it for attention,' so he cut up his whole arm to show everyone else that this wasn't the case. Then he came here. Do you think if you do that people's minds will change? Sure, they might be surprised at first. But do you think it would change how they feel about you? What are they going to say after you make a point of how bad things were for you, 'Oh, how much you must've suffered'? Is there really a difference whether you show them or not, in the end?

Me: Wouldn't they change their minds about me?

Psychiatrist: I'm saying there's a chance they were already thinking that before to some extent. I'm saying you can go on leave without stamping a big scarlet letter on yourself. You have to practise saying that you feel unwell when you feel unwell. Instead of enduring it until the last minute and going, 'Look at how much I've managed to endure, to the point of harming myself.'

Me: But what would change at the office if I told them I was sick?

Psychiatrist: I was just using an example. If you're at the stage of trying to decide whether you will continue at the office or not, you must've come to that point after much deliberation. But my impression is that whenever you do this deliberating, you just accept the circumstances. That instead of saying, 'I don't like this' or asserting your views, you just accept the situation.

Me: But if I don't accept the situation? I don't have any other choice.

Psychiatrist: You're the one who decided to think that way—

Me: (*Explodes*) But it's my job to make books, that's literally my profession, how could I just say I don't want to do that? Then what would happen, if a person whose job it was to make books went around saying she couldn't make books?

Psychiatrist: The creation of a book is not just one activity but a collection of different activities, and your job is a totality of solving different problems, but what if you've been simply accepting all of those problems?

Me: I don't know what I would do about that. I just want to quit.

Psychiatrist: I told you this over the phone as well, but I think you are in crisis mode. Even I can see that. But if your method of getting out of this crisis is to harm yourself, you're not going to really solve the problem. Sure, it'll feel great if you could just shout, *I quit*. But what would that be? Being swept along without having any control over your direction.

Me: I'm not being swept along by anything; I really just want to quit . . .

Psychiatrist: All right. If you want to quit, at least wait until you are feeling more like yourself, but until then I think it would be wise if you were put in a less stressful situation for the time being.

Me: Like in a hospital?

Psychiatrist: I think checking yourself in would be a good idea. I think you need it right now. The stress you're receiving from your daily life is so overwhelming that I believe it is impossible for you to try changing your perspective or thinking different thoughts right now. It's not that checking into a hospital will make the world around you happier and brighter. In fact, it won't, at all. But it will allow you to slow down a bit. You went on your trip to do just that, but here you are still stressed. I think you can consider quitting after you're out of the hospital. When it rains we put on raincoats or open an umbrella, but when it's really storming and blowing, none of that is effective anymore and we have to seek shelter.

Me: (*Couldn't say anything to that.*) Does the medicine give you hives?

Psychiatrist: Did you take out the pill I told you to take out?

Me: Only yesterday. There are hives all over my body, down my legs.

Psychiatrist: You should've taken that pill out. I told you the last time, but you're drinking and doing things that harm your body. You have a choice. It may hurt your pride a little, but I want to take that choice away from you. Even if it means putting you in the hospital to do so. You can't drink when you're in the hospital, so I'm hoping you'll have the urge to get better and leave. If getting drunk solved your problems or opened the next stage in your growth, then I would tell you to get drunk. But drinking solves nothing when you get up the next morning. If the situation is so unbearable that you can't go on, you shouldn't try to go on by cutting yourself, but tell someone, 'I'm really having a hard time, I want to rest for a bit, I'll take the long way.' I want you to be brave enough to do that. You can make the decision after you've toured the facilities, and if you don't like them I hope you consider a university hospital. My thought is that you should check yourself in and think of nothing for a few days.

Me: Can I read a book?

Psychiatrist: You can take a book in with you.

Me: I just have to call and ask if I can check in?

Psychiatrist: The doctor makes that decision, so you'd have to be examined. And you should check to see if they have a ward available.

Me: I'll call them. I think I can check in right now.

Psychiatrist: Yes, you can go anytime. It's fine to go now.

Me: All right.

Psychiatrist: I'll write up a referral for you to show them. I don't think it's helpful to provide too much information, anyway. It's much

better for them to talk with you directly, but
if they need further consultation, ask them to
call me.

Me: I will.

THE DESIRE TO BE BOTH ME AND NOT ME

'Was this your first self-harming incident?'

After the consultation, I received a prescription and a referral. I went right to a hospital and checked myself in. When it was my turn there was a woman doctor who asked me questions in a dry tone. *Were you drunk, was this your first self-harming incident, how did you feel?* I was told to leave for a moment and to send in my guardian. My partner went in, then after a long while, came back out and said maybe it would be better if we left. I asked them why, and they said it was because this wasn't a place where I could rest comfortably, that it was somewhere that cut me off completely and managed every hour of my day. That there were people here in worse conditions who might stress out patients like me. That what I needed was to quit drinking and my job. That quitting drinking was the most important thing. I came home and dumped all the beer down the drain. I didn't even think about drinking. My partner kept whispering to me about my shining future yet to come (that might never come) in very firm stories that had clear, inevitable structures. They whispered these to me until I fell asleep.

I took an indefinite sick leave. Like I was hit with a sleeping disease, I just slept day and night. Time seemed to creep after I'd harmed myself. In the end, I want to be myself and not myself at the same time, always. I don't know where this strange contradiction will lead me.

5

BECAUSE I FEAR BOTH LIVING AND DYING

Sitting there at home doing nothing, staring out the rectangle of light that was the window, listening to children play and the spring breeze blow – it all made me experience the passage of time; a sensation I hadn't felt in a long while. I thought about self-harm. I was scared at first that this was the first step towards suicide, but then I wondered if this was actually my struggle to survive (because, as contradictory as it may sound, I wanted to live as much as I wanted to die). I really wanted to die, and that desire was so large it was slowly accumulating inside my body, and the only way to let that desire loose was to harm myself. It wasn't enough to just cry and drink. I felt a release after harming myself, and hoped that the next day would be better. It's not the healthiest way to prevent myself from suicide, but I was finding it hard to find an alternative.

Psychiatrist: You didn't check yourself in? Did you go to the hospital?

Me: I went. But it was a completely shut-off hospital . . . they said it wasn't like taking a break inside and that I could end up feeling more stressed, so I went home.

Psychiatrist: Without even taking a look?

Me: Yes.

Psychiatrist: You knew it was a closed ward before you went, but hearing that made you change your mind?

Me: I was just so tired all I wanted was to sleep. I wanted to sleep, but they put you on a programme that starts in the morning and keeps you occupied . . . I just wasn't feeling well, so I went home and slept for three days.

Psychiatrist: What did you do after sleeping?

Me: I was at home. Aside from taking the dogs out for a walk, I didn't go anywhere.

Psychiatrist: Did it feel pleasant to take the walk?

Me: It was, but I did think the feeling would be temporary.

Psychiatrist: What did you do for food?

Me: I didn't miss a meal.

Psychiatrist: What did you think about while you rested at home?

Me: Well . . . I think I alternated between good days and bad, but the day after I self-harmed, I felt a bit better. I felt a release. The day after that wasn't so good. I felt helpless, and during the day I tortured myself over my old wound. I thought I was going crazy. That sitting around here like this was only going to make me more crazy, that I needed to do something if I wanted to get better and I knew what I needed to do but I couldn't do that particular thing? All those feelings. I began feeling better yesterday afternoon. I felt good yesterday, but I don't feel well again.

Psychiatrist: Do you feel it's going to be a good day or bad the moment you open your eyes? Or does it happen when you're doing something?

Me: My condition is what it is from the moment I open my eyes.

Psychiatrist: You know how you judge the weather when you open your eyes in the morning? How did you feel when the sun was coming up?

Me: I hated it. So much. Because I have really bad eczema right now and hives all over my body. But our place doesn't have blackout curtains, so all of that light just comes inside. It hits my skin directly. I hate it so much I use the smaller bedroom where the blinds come down and I wear long pyjamas to hide myself.

Psychiatrist: Do you reflexively look at your skin when the sun comes up?

Me: Yes. And I immediately think how much I hate it.

Psychiatrist: Is the state of your skin getting worse?

Me: I've cut off alcohol cold turkey because they said my drinking was the biggest problem. It's been about a week since I've had a drink. But when I self-harmed this last time, it was broad daylight, and I was sober . . .

Psychiatrist: How did that feel? Did it feel like the first time?

Me: I don't know. Doing it once made me think it wasn't a big deal. And I didn't scratch myself too deeply, so it scabs over quickly and then falls off without any scarring? I didn't want to lose the wound, which is why I repeatedly scratched over those spots. There's also this: I'm going to go into the office and tell them I'm not doing well, so wouldn't it be better if I had these scars to prove my point?

Psychiatrist: How do you think they will react when you tell them you're quitting? What is the value in proving your point by showing them your wounds?

Me: There's a procedure to quitting. Even after you declare it, there's a month grace period. You have to pass your work on to the next person. But I was thinking I could speed things up if I showed them my wounds. My company has this very complicated resignation process. Lots of paperwork.

Psychiatrist: I see. Is there any period during your day when you feel better?

Me: When I open my eyes in the morning, I have this particular feeling, you know? Either of being weighed down by helplessness or being very light and clear. That first feeling determines the rest of my day. It never varies from that.

Psychiatrist: Then does it persist on your good days as well?

Me: Just because it's a good day, that doesn't mean I feel like it's great to be alive.

Psychiatrist: Does your mood change according to your skin condition?

Me: Yes, there's that, too. Things are getting better little by little, but my legs, for instance, are really bad, so normally it makes me feel worse.

Psychiatrist: And the wound on your arm is getting better?

Me: Yes. Little by little.

Psychiatrist: Aside from taking your dogs out for a walk, was there anything in particular you did inside the house?

Me: Normally, I don't watch TV. But I got addicted to this show, *Produce 101*, which is about idols. There's this boy, Daniel Kang, who is really cute. I went into his fandom thinking it might help bring some colour into my life, but I do genuinely like the artist. I watched as many videos of him as possible, all the shows he appeared in. But it wasn't that fun. It felt a little empty, and I hated my life. Watching the shows made me feel a bit better. Because they were funny. Immersing myself in something funny made me feel better.

Psychiatrist: Your partner could see your wounds. What was their reaction to them?

Me: It pains them, they cry. A lot. They feel guilty that they couldn't stop me from it. And I feel sorry about that.

Psychiatrist: Have you been in contact with anyone else other than your partner?

Me: Not at all. Oh wait, doctor, a friend of mine sent me a KakaoTalk message, and I'm in such a state these days that I didn't answer or even look at it. But then they must've felt slighted or were desperate because they began to send a flurry of messages. I didn't read them, but . . . I really hated that. But if that friend is depending on me and I cast them off, they'll be hurt. So I just end up doing nothing about the situation.

Psychiatrist: This is part of the pattern. Instead of thinking about this person, try to focus on the now. Wouldn't it be better if you simply thought, 'Things are hard for me right now, and I'm sorry but I don't have the bandwidth to worry about you or help you, I'll answer you later'?

Me: Oh wait, that's all I need to do? It's weird how I keep having these silly thoughts. I wanted to die so much, and I thought of you as well. How guilty would my doctor feel if I killed myself, that kind of thing? But doctor, I'm being honest here and not overdramatic, but if I truly don't want to live – what am I going to do? I really don't want to go on.

I'm sure someone listening to me now would think, 'Why does she bother continuing to live, why doesn't she just die,' right?

Psychiatrist: I don't think you're being overdramatic at all. And you've been wanting to die for a while, not just today.

Me: (*Bursts into tears.*) I just, I don't know. My life before I took medication has become the past, and I can just forget the memories of that time, but I think I'm getting worse. So I keep castigating myself, and because I'm so mired in it and keep thinking of myself as sick, I'm making the sickness even worse, which makes me feel like it's all too much. And this drives me up the wall, which makes me think of harming myself. I'm usually a coward and would never give in to the urge, but you know how you do something once and realise it's not such a big deal? When I got to thinking, 'Ah, it really isn't a big deal,' I just started to cut without thinking too much about it.

Psychiatrist: I know things are hard for you right now, and that you want to die. That's why I recommended you check yourself in. Although I wonder if they didn't quite understand my intentions at that hospital.

Me: The hospital said there were lots of people like me. That if someone like me comes in, I wouldn't even last a day . . . they kept saying that, which made me think I'd be better off resting at home.

Psychiatrist: But your rest at home isn't quite rest, either. Think back to how you were before you took medication. Think of how much better your life was after you started on your pills, you were much better off than now. That was about a month ago.

Me: You're right. Do you think this depression, this helplessness, decreases interest or curiosity or fun in life?

Psychiatrist: Yes. It destroys all interest in life.

Me: I know this isn't the best way to describe it, but I feel like an old woman who has seen everything. I'm not interested in anything anymore, and I tried to really get into the Daniel Kang of it all, but today I just lost interest. Everything loses its shine, I can't fully immerse myself in anything anymore, and nothing is fun. The odd thing is, though, while I still feel that my life is boring, I really want to do something. This past week was full of rest, and I had loads of time. I spent three days of it asleep, and even with four hours of watching television, I was still left with so much time. I want to get rid of all this time, or boredom, really, and I have to do something to do that, right? But I feel helpless. Bored, but also without energy. This keeps repeating itself and I feel like I'm going to lose my mind. So I go out at midnight and lay down on the grass in the park. Because I feel like I'm suffocating. Whatever my condition is that day, I still feel like I need to do something, but my helplessness prevents me from doing anything. It's possible if I'm feeling good that day. Like yesterday, which was a pleasant day. I watched the sunset in the evening, ran around with the dogs, smelled the flowers. I felt like life was worth living yesterday evening, for a brief time. But just a day later I could slip into helplessness, it's like black and white. I'm completely disinterested in the world around me. They say you should look for the simple pleasures of life, but who doesn't know that? I'm saying it's hard to do even that . . . I feel like I'm broken, and to go on living like this would be a horrifying thing.

Psychiatrist: I agree that living like this is a horrible thing. But on the other hand, how long can such a state continue? You're thinking that you cannot improve beyond this point, that if you have a good day, it will inevitably be followed by a bad one. But what if that weren't the case? What if you looked back and counted the number of days you felt this way and the number of those you didn't? You feel that you are stuck in one place. I can't guarantee you will change, but there are many people in emergency rooms who have tried to slice their wrists like you have, or people who come here after having failed in their attempts. They have different attitudes when they are discharged from the hospital. They all say: 'Why did I only think in that way back then . . .?'

Me: It really is like that; I really did feel better the day after self-harm. Like, why did I do that? I'm crazy, I should get healthier, stop drinking and eat properly and exercise! And then the next day, I'm helpless again. And I cut myself.

Psychiatrist: I think the changes you feel day to day seem more negative to you than they actually are. You'll remember you told me you felt good a month ago. What's happened in the month since? That's probably playing a large role in how you feel now.

Me: The book thing, the eczema, the weight.

Psychiatrist: It's not a question of whether you're publishing a book or not but the things you are able to do in the process of publishing a book and the things that are out of your control that you might not even be aware of . . . I think that second category may be influencing your feelings a lot.

Me: Can things I'm not really aware of stress me out regardless?

Psychiatrist: Of course.

Me: The hospital I went to also suggested I quit my job.

Psychiatrist: It's just that your feelings about your work are a little *too* negative.

Me: Doctor, to be honest with you, I want to throw up every time I think about going to work. I really think I should quit.

Psychiatrist: As I told you before, you can always quit. But what if that turns out to be a decision you made when unwell and then you regret it later?

Me: I do think I would say yes to taking a leave of absence if it were possible, for about a month? But then I think to myself that if the company gives me a month off, I'll have that much more of a debt to them, and I would have to work without complaining once I return, but what happens if I feel unwell again? And (*I think for the hundredth time*) what if I'm just making a fuss over nothing . . .

Psychiatrist: That's because you keep looking at the world from other peoples' perspectives.

Me: Yes, yes. But I see myself as making a fuss, which is why I think other people are thinking the same thing.

Psychiatrist: It's hardly nothing. You had a flare-up of your skin condition, work wasn't going so well, and your carefully created plan wasn't panning out, which is stressful. All of these things must've stimulated your fear of what others might think.

Me: Yes, exactly. It was very much like that. It's been four to five months since switching from marketing to editorial, and I feel so incompetent. I have no good ideas, no confidence. Those thoughts keep dominating my thinking, which makes me hate work. And I keep comparing myself to others. People who write better than I do, who get more attention, it doesn't matter which gender they are, I compare myself to them. The ridiculous thing is, I'm watching Daniel Kang and envying him. Like, wow he's so young and cool and is enjoying life and is all sparkly. Just, envy.

Psychiatrist: I think such comparisons aren't truly about comparing yourself to anyone, but are a tool for trying to emphasise your sense of inferiority.

Me: Really? I think I have such a strong sense of inferiority.

Psychiatrist: That's not surprising. If you really loved yourself, why would you feel like you want to die? It's the same with one's abilities. Just like one has no motivation or doesn't want to do anything when depressed, the condition of depression also impacts mental abilities. You have lower concentration, your memory deteriorates and you score lower on IQ exams when depressed.

Me: Really? It's so hard for me to read for long periods. I feel like the words evaporate from the page. Which is why I haven't been reading lately.

Psychiatrist: I want you to stop doing everything that you feel obligated to do. But I want you to think about what you normally like doing, and try at least pretending to do those things while depressed. It matters less if you do them on good days.

Me: I've felt this for sure this time, but I think I really don't know anything about myself (*this again*). I don't know if it's because I'm stupid, but I don't know what I'm good at or what I like, I just feel like there's nothing. I just like my dogs. They're the only thing. I just keep them close.

Psychiatrist: It's even harder to think of such things when you're unwell. In that state, thinking about what you normally like could make you feel bad as well. Like pressure. For example, when you're down, you could meet someone who's in a worse condition and comfort them, feeling like you're better off in the process. But what actually happens is that you see that person and think, 'I shouldn't be so sad when there are people who are worse off . . . I should be feeling happy right now,' essentially continuing to punish yourself.

Me: You're right. I keep doing that. 'Who do you think you are that you get to be so depressed?' I ask myself that all the time. And the fact that I can't think of an answer makes it worse.

Psychiatrist: Do you have an appetite when you're feeling good?

Me: I always have an appetite. When I sit down to eat, at least. Isn't this a cypress? (*Points at potted plant.*) I think I should go now.

Psychiatrist: I'm going to adjust your dosage. These daily highs and lows in your mood seem a bit too severe to be simply depression, so I'm going to increase your medication, but gradually, because doing it all at once isn't good for you. And telling yourself to look at the sky, take in the sun, all of that is good for you, but I don't want you to punish yourself harshly for not doing those things either. When making yourself go out once a day, try doing so at a time that's convenient for you. It's a good idea to buy blackout curtains as well. I hope you also attempt to get better on a physical level.

Me: Thank you, doctor. I'll see you next week.

THE HABIT OF HELPLESSNESS

'The plant looks fine, but it's already dying, past the point of no return.'

I ended up quitting my job. I thought I would get better if I took an open-ended break from work, but nothing changed. One day, I just told my company that I was quitting. Having swiftly passed on my duties to others, I was surprised to find some of my colleagues in tears as I said my goodbyes. I'd believed they had only thought of me as some overdramatic, overprivileged nut who was making life harder for everyone else, but apparently that wasn't the case. Why on earth did I think I was harming them by being there? In any case, having quit my job, I now had so much time and no idea what to do with myself.

When I woke up this morning, the sunlight flooded my vision. I hated it. Waking up around 7 wasn't such a shock to the eyes, but at 8.30, the light was an assault. The hives and scars on my skin make my irritation spike. I scroll through Instagram. Someone I'm jealous of is always meeting someone I don't know, going to places I've never heard of, listening to music I'm not familiar with. This feeling of being left behind, or that this person is special while I am not. Their posts are always so interesting, their expressions fresh, but what am I? Neither here nor there, which I hate.

Then I walked the dogs, flooding myself with serotonin, and that let me change my mindset slightly. Like, at least the skin on my face is fine. I shouldn't force myself to do anything about something that's beyond my control. And what I fear the most is helplessness. It's crucial to keep myself occupied if I want to get over something, but helplessness brings me down in that regard too. Being helpless makes me feel like a plant that's been ripped out at the roots. The plant looks fine, but it's already dying, past the point of no return.

As I sit with my dogs in my arms, I hear the spring breeze blowing and children playing, and see the cherry blossoms and the forsythia wilting and falling. I want to lie down in the sun for a while. To feel the season, even for just a few minutes, right down to my very bones. Because summer is coming soon. I want to be healthy.

6

THAT SOMEONE WISHES FOR
MY SAFETY

I was in a car accident. It was my first time driving from Hongdae and Gwanghwamun back to Ilsan, and it was on this final leg at Ilsan. I was at the point on the highway where you merge with the cars turning right, but it was one of those intersections where the merge happens immediately after the turn, and I hadn't checked for oncoming traffic. There was a loud honk and I crashed into an oncoming truck, my small car shaking violently. The cars filing behind the truck came to a stop under the traffic light at the crossing.

As my car halted, all I could think was that I was done for, but there were people opening my driver-side and passenger-side doors, checking to see if I was all right. They said they'd been fearful I was seriously injured. I was in complete shock, and passersby called for an ambulance and the police. By the grace of the heavens, I was physically unharmed – but I had to scrap the car. The wounds on my wrist and the crumpled-up car made me wonder if a person's fate was indeed something set, that you were not supposed to go if it wasn't your time. Maybe, I thought, it's not that easy for me to die. And in that moment, seeing how many people there were who were struggling to live for one more day, my worries seemed especially petty and almost luxurious, which made me hate myself.

Psychiatrist: How have you been?

Me: I was in a car accident . . . I had to dump my car. I hit a truck but miraculously was unscathed.

Psychiatrist: What a relief! But you say it so casually.

Me: Yes . . . that's basically how it happened. I'm glad I'm all right. I was not in a good state up until yesterday. I ran out of prescription meds two days ago. But once I got my meds refilled, my headache and depression lessened. When I kept taking my pills on time, I hadn't been too aware of their effect (*because I was used to them*), but once I'd skipped a few days, I felt extremely bad. I think if I'd had appointments with you during the days I didn't take my meds, I wouldn't have been able to keep them.

Psychiatrist: Do you feel the urge to get another tattoo these days?

Me: Not these days. Just strong urges to self-harm. But I think the accident yesterday had an effect. I had been out and about – I went to a bookstore near Hongdae and to Kyobo in Gwanghwamun, driving all the way despite my being a beginner driver and how difficult the routes are. I had successfully returned to

Ilsan, got my prescription, and was on my way home when the accident happened.

Whenever I drove in Seoul, I kept imagining myself crashing into the side of a hill or a wall. I kept crying while I drove, too. And because it takes a lot of courage to crash into something myself, I'd hoped someone would crash into me instead. But then yesterday it actually happened. At a point where I was supposed to merge, where if I'd gone in just half a second earlier, the driver's side would've been completely smashed. But instead, everything *but* the driver's seat was smashed. It was my partner's car, too.

I'd never been in an accident before and had no idea how serious this crash was, but passersby apparently were convinced I was dead from the way I had hit the truck and then a streetlamp. They came running up to me and opening the doors and trying to help me. I was in too much shock to do anything while they called 119 and 112 for me. The truck driver was so afraid I was dead that they couldn't even bring themselves to come up to the car. But I'm fine. I have to wait and see if there are any after-effects, but aside from that, I feel all right.

You know how I feel so bored with my daily life? And unaware of how lucky I am in that ordinariness? I was feeling more bored than ever the last few days, especially with having to stay home all the time. But after surviving yesterday's accident and having that stroke of luck, I thought, 'I guess it's not my time to die, I guess there's still something left I need to do' and that made me feel, I don't know, grateful? I have this old dog, you know, Juding, who lives with my family in Ilsan. I was taking Juding in the car to my home in Paju when the accident happened. I was so grateful we both survived, and coming home to both my dogs and remembering how the pedestrians came running to help me made me think, 'How grateful I am in this moment, that I can see all of this with my own eyes.'

Psychiatrist: You couldn't think of such things before then?

Me: I couldn't. I was just filled with my own darkness. I took what was precious to me for granted and shoved it all in a corner of my heart. I was so bored with the present and kept going over the past, or the past kept recurring in my mind. I couldn't enjoy the present. My exes, I would also get bored of them. There was one I was in contact with for a bit, but they started going out with someone new.

And that made me feel bad for some reason. I happened upon some of our old emails and rereading them made me feel sad.

Psychiatrist: You felt like you wanted to see them again?

Me: Not really, I was just feeling sad in the moment. The last thing they had said to me was, 'I hope you learn how to enjoy the present. It's not that your past isn't meaningful, and I don't know what your partner now is like, but I get the feeling that if you put your best into the present, you'll feel the same way I do now. I really hope you'll be happy.' It brought tears to my eyes. And I told them, all right, I'll try to be true to the moment. And then the accident happened, and my partner came running and the first thing they checked was whether I was OK, and seeing them feel genuinely happy because I was unharmed was really moving to me. It made me think I truly was the only person who was being pathetic and silly, and I swore I would do right by them. Oh, and we scrapped the car and decided to buy a new one with my severance pay.

Psychiatrist: Swearing to do right? Oh, you mean to be true to the present. But also, I really hope you get a full hospital check-up at some point.

Me: I will.

Psychiatrist: Death has always shadowed you and you've wished to die recently, but now that you've experienced near-death, have you been feeling that you're glad you didn't die then?

Me: Not gladness, really. When it happened, I didn't immediately think, 'I'm glad I survived and didn't get hurt.' I got out of the car and looked at the car and could tell it was headed to the scrapyard. Instead of feeling glad I survived I thought, 'This is my partner's car, what are they going to say? Oh no, I'm dead.' I didn't really value my own life, in other words. I even thought it might have been better if I'd died.

Psychiatrist: The fact that you had that worry at all is proof you're alive.

Me: Oh, I see. Anyway, I didn't really feel glad I was alive, but it did feel like I died and was reborn yesterday. Like it was a turning point? I've no idea how long this will last.

Psychiatrist: But this was such a significant experience that I think you need to ruminate over it a bit more. I mean, you ruminate quite a bit to begin with. Those wishes you had before the accident (*I want to be in an accident, I want someone to run into me*) became real, and you saw how it doesn't just end like that – there were other things that happened afterwards. Or perhaps you might be in pain later, even if you don't feel anything now.

Me: Right. Like if I had hurt my back, my life going forward would be so hard for me . . .

Psychiatrist: Remember how we changed your dosage a bit last week? I raised it. And there were pills for your headache.

Me: Yes, my headache immediately disappeared.

Psychiatrist: Keep taking those pills. The other medication is actually for bipolar disorder. Those feelings of extremes that come and go may be a condition you've had since birth. Everyone has their weak points. With you, I think you're not as good at regulating your emotions. So I upped your mood regulators a bit.

Me: Oh, I did feel my emotions were a lot less up and down yesterday, actually. It was a peace I hadn't felt in a long time, I was so happy. It was good.

Psychiatrist: Your accident may have had a big effect.

Me: I think so. A release of sorts.

Psychiatrist: When our stability transforms into boredom, we preoccupy ourselves with all sorts of random thoughts. Like you said, we could think about our former partners, compare the present to the past. But if you injure yourself, your thoughts will concentrate on your injury. You don't have the wherewithal to think of anything else after an accident. Because of shock and guilt and all that.

Me: That's true. I haven't even had headaches since the accident. I can't feel a thing anywhere in my body.

Psychiatrist: This may simply be the mood you are in now. It could be a blessing. Or a curse. But after an accident, you may find yourself thinking of your old worries and complaints as luxuries.

Me: Right. Even more so if I'd been seriously injured.

Psychiatrist: Exactly. You could've sustained permanent injuries to your body and mind. You were very, very lucky. Things could've been so much worse. You might've thought you wanted to die because of your injuries.

Me: Yes, yes. Those old thoughts were luxuries . . . I'm so grateful to not be injured, for the response of the people around me.

Psychiatrist: I hope you take care of yourself better and don't stop at gratitude.

Me: I really should.

Psychiatrist: You've said before that you're numb to pain and suffering. I think, precisely because of that, you should be ever more sensitive to your own health. Especially now, post-accident.

Me: I shall. And you know how I was wild about Daniel Kang when I wasn't feeling well? I actually had a crush on him. I wanted to go out with him (*how silly of me*). I was ashamed of these feelings, I wanted to hide them. But there's this novel titled, *Phantom Pain*. It's about why fans fall in love with idols. It's a really good novel. It made me think, I already consider homosexuality, asexuality, polyamory, etc. as valid forms of love, but why was I so disrespectful of a fan's love for their idol? Who cares if I had a crush on a celebrity, as long as I'm not going up to them in person and harming them? That's the thought I had. But I also had these other thoughts when I liked him, heartbreaking thoughts. That I liked him so much as I watched his videos and listened to his music and bought everything associated with him, but he didn't even know

I existed, which made me feel so much pain over unrequited love. At least when you have a crush on a real person, they know about it. Or at least, they might know about it. But this love was the kind that could never come true. Which made me a bit depressed.

Psychiatrist: It's exactly as you just said: there are many ways of loving. It's like religion. One might think of someone else's religion, 'Oh, that's problematic,' but to the person immersed in their religion, it may just be a desperate desire to reach something. You said you felt a bit depressed, but that passion you felt could lead to other things. A desire for a celebrity could spur you to meet someone new, or make friends with other fans, and all of these are meaningful connections and relationships.

Me: You're right. I think that's it for now.

Psychiatrist: Rest well and sweet dreams, I'll see you next week.

Me: Thank you so much. Have a great weekend!

THE DAY THE THINGS I TOOK FOR GRANTED SEEMED NEW

'Maybe there was some purpose left in me.'

You never know what's going to happen in life. The future is impossible to predict, even if that future is only a second away. A scary but fascinating truth. When my accident happened, I neither thought I was going to die nor considered the accident itself as a major one. To the point where, because it wasn't my car that was totalled, I thought it would've been better if I'd died instead of facing the consequences.

But I escaped without a scratch. I was so unharmed it was almost ridiculous. Unharmed despite having hit a truck, having totalled my partner's car.

It made me look upon my life anew, with a fresh set of eyes. The things I'd taken for granted suddenly seemed very clear and true. Not because I lived, but because I didn't die. This may sound strange, but I really felt it wasn't my time to go. I thought: maybe there was some purpose left in me. I wanted to believe that, and to pursue it.

7

THE ANNIVERSARY

Sunday was our anniversary. A joyful day where we were supposed to see a musical and have a meal at a fancy restaurant, which was why my partner and I really wanted me to maintain a positive outlook. I was careful not to fall into a negative mood, as it would be difficult to get out of it once I was in it.

After reading several critical reviews that verged on harsh insults, I had completely avoided reviews of my first book. But early that morning, for a reason I could not fathom, I went on Twitter and searched the title of my book. There were many positive reviews that made me think, 'Wow, I guess Twitter was always the best audience for my writing after all!', but as I scrolled down further, I came across what was probably the nastiest review I had read yet. To paraphrase, it went something like: *I feel like I've just survived a disease. Why don't you keep these thoughts to yourself in your Hello Kitty diary next time? To charge money for people to read these thoughts, it goes beyond disgusting into evil. Trash.*

Psychiatrist: How have you been?

Me: I had a good week.

Psychiatrist: How was it good?

Me: It was generally positive, but there was an incident. (*I describe what happened as above.*) But I didn't want to ruin that day. I was about to say to my partner, 'Console me at once!' but I went outside with the dogs instead. And I tried out this new method I thought of, which is having a conversation with myself. I said, 'Hey Sehee, you're not Jesus or Buddha, and even you sometimes hate a book, even the classics, right? So why should everyone in the world enjoy your book?' and I answered, 'I guess you're right,' to which I said, 'And do you find there are more people messaging you about how they like your book or reviews like this saying how much they hate it?' and I replied, 'I guess there are more people who say they like it.' Then, 'So why do you think so little of people's opinions when they say they like your book and make such a big deal of the opinions that say they hate it? Isn't that just bad manners, denigrating your readers like that? Don't you feel you've gotten a little entitled?' And I said, 'Right, I guess it's a bit arrogant of me,' and then, 'And think about it. Don't you realise that person on Twitter must've picked up the book at a bookshop and determined whether it was for them or not in the first place? In other words, isn't it weird of them to be so harsh about a book they picked out with their own hands?' I replied, 'You know what, you're right. They *are* being weird. I'm not going to think about them anymore.' And I felt completely at peace after that.

Psychiatrist: Have you heard of this book—

Me: Which book?

Psychiatrist: —titled *Psychodrama*?

Me: Me? No.

Psychiatrist: It's a bit similar to the psychodramatic method.

Me: Really? There's a therapeutic method where you have a conversation with yourself? I didn't just imagine the conversation in my head; I actually had a talk with myself. And it really felt like I was having a conversation, even though it was only with myself.

Psychiatrist: This method of questioning and answering allows you to see things you hadn't initially seen when you were too upset to take note.

Me: You're right. It really felt like an emotionally charged me and a rational, objective me were having a conversation. I felt much calmer after having this ping-pong game of a dialogue. Not fake calm but *really* calm, too. I was actually, really, all right. On our way to the musical, I told my partner about it, that there was this incident and I handled it this way, that I felt completely fine now, and my partner said I was really amazing, that they would find it difficult to do the same thing themselves. I was so happy about everything. We had a really nice day. And I realised something. A lot of readers recently have been sending me messages about how much they like the book, right? I was really moved by them at first. I basically wrote that book because of a single positive comment on a blog post, but even that gratitude wears thin after a while. I mean, I've felt grateful for the support, but I was kind of taking it for granted. This incident made me chastise myself and reread those messages with a grateful attitude.

Psychiatrist: You've returned to your initial mindset? That's good news.

Me: Yes. But this method, it really exists?

Psychiatrist: It's quite popular. Sometimes in dramatised form, where they sit a bunch of people down and they all speak from your perspective. But hearing your story, I wonder if the answer was there all along. You know how you thought, 'Wow, I guess Twitter is my crowd!' or some such, right? It might be helpful to think of the mean person, 'That person is not going to enjoy Twitter.' And they might've written that comment just for the sake of dissenting. Thinking that the contrarian view would make them seem cool and different. (*This strikes me as rationalisation.*)

Me: I guess so. There wasn't anything special going on besides this incident. I do want to ask you something. A lot of people are asking me about getting treatment. And there's one thing people tend to wonder about. You know how I have sessions with you that last thirty or forty minutes at a time? They want to know if it's common for a psychiatrist, not a psychological counsellor, to conduct such sessions.

Psychiatrist: It is indeed not common.

Me: Really? May I ask why you do it, then?

Psychiatrist: Well, when you started seeing me, you happened to catch me at a moment when I had more time than usual. When a patient seems to need a bit of time to discuss things, I try to accommodate them. And I'm not good at cutting into people talking and making them summarise their points.

Me: And you don't. Cut in when I talk, I mean.

Psychiatrist: I'm really bad at that. Of course, when I have too many patients to see, I have to do it.

Me: You're right. Our sessions are timed for half an hour, which makes me conscious of the time and I keep checking the clock. (*But in many cases, the doctor is the one who keeps talking and going over time.*)

Psychiatrist: And every patient has different needs that require different solutions. There are cases where a patient lives so far away it takes them an hour to get here, but their session is over in five minutes. The patient is itching to get away, in other words. And it also depends on how much the patient is willing to open up.

Me: You know how some people might be afraid of opening up, but they still bravely manage to make their way to you? And somehow they have to go through this questioning and answering process with you if they want to deal with their problems, but they can't bear to open their mouths? How do you help them?

Psychiatrist: If the patient in question does not trust in therapy, there is nothing I can do for them. No matter how much their friends and family encourage them to get help, all they have to do is sit there and say, 'I'm fine,' and that's that. And on the not-being-able-to-open-their-mouths thing: the silence sometimes needs to be waited out. I tend to think of silence as another mode of conversation. It depends on the disorder, of course. Especially with psychiatry, there are discussions that are possible only when a certain rapport is present. And there are things that could never be discussed no matter what.

Me: Then there are people who say just one or two words and they're out of here?

Psychiatrist: They do exist.

Me: And are there people who build rapport and eventually begin to open up?

Psychiatrist: Yes, there are such cases. And others who prefer to just receive prescriptions. And still others who are even more active than I am in talking. There is such a variety of cases that it's impossible to generalise.

Me: Then would a patient call you beforehand to ask if the session will last ten minutes or thirty?

Psychiatrist: The important thing is that the patient has to be able to handle what is being discussed. For example, from a psychiatrist's point of view, telling a patient their prognosis for the sake of early intervention can actually come as a huge shock to a patient who is not ready to hear it. Especially when they're suffering heavily from their symptoms.

Me: You try to judge if that's the case?

Psychiatrist: I do. Not that I manage to catch every patient at the right time to make that determination. In any case, I think it's tricky to say how long a session would last absolutely, but maybe they could ask how long the first session might be? (*Isn't that what I meant in the first place . . .?*)

Me: Got it.

THE SILENCE

'I want to be able to meet my darker emotions on their own terms.'

The idea that silence was part of the process of therapy gave me pause. As did the fact that, of the countless people suffering from depression, only a fraction manage to make themselves get treatment.

Certain people who read my book commented that I am a weak person who seems to kick up a lot of fuss. That was saddening. The thing is, I've been consoled by a particular book about suffering. That is Viktor Frankl's *Man's Search for Meaning*, the true account of the author's survival of the Auschwitz Nazi death camp. It was hard to read in the beginning because it made me wonder why it was so hard for me to go through life when here was someone who had survived much worse. Frankl himself writes that 'suffering completely fills the human soul and conscious mind, no matter whether the suffering is great or little. Therefore the "size" of human suffering is absolutely relative.'

I've stopped comparing my suffering to that of others, which has enabled me to seek professional help instead of just enduring it on my own. As hard as it is to avoid, using the standards of society and others to measure and suppress one's own suffering is a very dangerous exercise. I want to be able to meet my darker emotions on their own terms. Just as we immerse ourselves in our own enjoyment, I want to look into my own darkness and have a conversation with it, and to comfort myself.

8

WIDEN THAT MIDDLE GROUND WITHIN ME

Psychiatrist: How have you been?

Me: All right. A couple of bad days, but I got over them right away.

Psychiatrist: Why were those days bad?

Me: There were clear reasons. I did an interview with a newspaper, and I was so grateful when the journalist came all the way to Paju to do it. He sounded young on the phone, but he turned out to be middle-aged in person. This was disconcerting. Until now, my interviews had been conducted by young female journalists and the vibes had been positive. And about eighty per cent of my reading audience happens to be women in their twenties and thirties, right? I might be a little prejudiced saying this, but I thought my book wouldn't be properly understood by a middle-aged man. And I was right.

Psychiatrist: In what way?

Me: Well, I don't know. Maybe I haven't met a great variety of people, but he was a bit intimidating. It's difficult to explain, but despite his very polite way of speaking, his behaviour was oddly condescending. I'd never met someone like that before; he confused me. 'Is this his way of being polite? Is it just his personality?' I was questioning things like that. But because I tend to think of myself as lacking in confidence and being oversensitive, I decided not to let that affect me. I just calmly answered his questions.

When I got back home and talked about the interview with a friend, I couldn't help thinking of what I had said, going back over it. There were quite a few questions that were a bit discourteous, but I simply assumed I was being too sensitive, as I told my friend. I thought they would go, 'Well, that seems like standard fare.' But my friend got all angry and said it sounded like the man had it in for me, that she would've walked out if she were me, that I had been so patient, so mature. That I did the right thing in being so polite and smart about it to the end.

But when she was saying those things, my mind went into a spiral. I'd been uncertain of his attitude and had not thought of him as a rude person, but I was suddenly overcome with the thought, 'Oh no, I've stupidly been unable to realise something again; he really had been insulting me, but like some idiot I hadn't recognised it and had given him all these polite answers.' My friend was thrown. She had meant to compliment me, but here I was, falling into self-hatred instead. She tried to explain that wasn't what she meant, but I was already too mired in my negative thoughts. You know how extreme I am, if I ever meet someone I don't like for some reason, I don't stop at 'What a weird person' but go straight to 'I hate all people!' So I spent that night crying and saying how much I hated all people, hated meeting people, and hugged my dogs close and said I was never going anywhere else ever again and fell asleep like that. I was filled with rage at the interviewer the next day as well. But then he sent me a text message saying, 'Send me four to five photos.' I texted him back, saying, 'When are you going to send me a draft of the interview?' and then he called me. As soon as I picked up, he said, 'Did I say I was going to send you a draft?' So I said, 'Every interview I've done before this has confirmed my quotes with me before going out.' He goes, 'I've been a journalist for twenty years and we've never done that even with the president', and how I should know better because I'd worked for a publisher for a long time. I was so upset. But hanging onto the last thread of my composure, I told him that I found him rude and upsetting and that I would prefer it if he didn't write this article. He said, 'Do you think I don't feel that way myself?' I replied that since neither of us felt good about it, he might as well not write it, and I hung up on him. I'd spent all the energy I had getting through that call, and I completely broke down after I hung up: I cried my eyes out. I felt so insulted. My publisher took care of it for me. They had a chat on the phone. I kept thinking I was being looked down on for being young and a woman, which tired me out, and I took a sleeping pill and went to sleep despite it being the middle of the day.

Psychiatrist: Did you take your evening pills then?

Me: I did. I took a sleeping pill in the day and slept, my evening pills in the evening, and I was about to take another sleeping pill at night but I felt sleepy anyway, so I didn't and went to bed. I had all sorts of nightmares. But they're all the same. I'm standing in front of someone unable to say what I really want to say in that moment like some loser, torturing myself. Even in my dreams I feel frustrated.

Psychiatrist: Why? When in reality you've said everything you wanted to say?

Me: If I think about it now, I do feel relieved having said everything I wanted to say in the moment, but . . . how do I explain this? I said what I wanted to say, but I was shaking and completely cowed by him at the same time. If we'd been talking in person, I wouldn't have been able to say a word.

Psychiatrist: Let's look at what you've told me about this journalist. He must've treated his interview subjects for the past twenty years just like he treated you, right? All that about never sending an interviewee a draft. But you then did exactly what you needed to do in that situation, which is completely different from what you did in your dream. The Sehee in your dream is just an idea of yourself.

It's not a bad thing at all that you heard what your friend said and thought, 'Hey, why didn't I think he was in the wrong and why did I misinterpret him as having good intentions? What's wrong with me?' But most people would've done what you did in the interview. They would've tried to make the best out of an uncomfortable situation. Being an adult is less about acting exactly the way you want just because you can, and more about trying to be patient in the midst of an infuriating situation. Plenty of people in this world try to go with the flow, to not rock the boat.

Me: And those people feel terrible when they lose their patience?

Psychiatrist: Yes. If you look at it from the perspective of people with power, they can bully whoever they want, right? But such people are criticised by society. And that's not the kind of person you want to be, am I wrong?

Me: No, you're right, absolutely.

Psychiatrist: But when such a person treated you in a way that made you feel looked down upon for being young, you still managed to keep your composure and maintain civility. It's not like you need to ever deal with him again for the rest of your life. You did what you were supposed to do and you did it well, but here you are castigating yourself for not expressing your emotions in the moment (*flying into a rage*), I just don't think that's fair on you.

Me: You're right. But doctor, I really feel like I'm doing better because I understood exactly what you meant when you said that just now. I'd been thinking about why I was like this, but honestly, being a bully and being criticised by society . . . that's not the life I want. But I keep thinking, 'I can't express myself properly, I'm a doormat for everyone to walk on.' Even when I'm not like that at all. And the past me isn't the real me anymore, but the bad me from the past convinces me, 'That's the real me!' Which makes me envious of the people who can't control their emotions and just let it all out. I sympathise with people who fly into a rage, and that becomes an ideal for me to aspire to. When it must be the opposite for most people . . .

Psychiatrist: It's probably the opposite for you, too.

Me: Really? But why am I like this?

Psychiatrist: When you're used to extremes, you can only perceive the other extreme from your current one. Youth is about going through difficulty; life itself is all about difficulty. But once you gain enough experience to see things less extremely, you realise there's a middle ground (*when am I ever going to find this middle ground?*), and when you grow older, you might even understand the seemingly cowardly act of compromise. But the most important thing is to find a way you are comfortable with. You're thinking in terms of 'I have to do this, I have to act like this' right now, but when time passes, you may begin thinking, 'I understand this side, and I understand the opposite side, but I'm more comfortable doing it like this.' I think you're already going in that direction. The next time you face a rude journalist, you'll be able to say to yourself, without any stirred-up emotion, 'That journalist was such a bore.' In any case, you handled that well.

Me: So you're saying that I think in extremes now so I idealise people who fly into rages?

Psychiatrist: Exactly. Because it's something that you don't do yourself. But the moment you turn that idealisation into action, you might find yourself castigating yourself and go, 'Why did I have to go that far?'

Me: Oh . . . I see. Something like that already happened. My partner and their friend and I were in a car together because our homes were in the same direction. The friend was a man, a big tall guy, and very short-tempered. He's not a bad person but somewhat impulsive, let's say. My partner was driving and an aggressive driver began screaming at us on the road. My partner was annoyed and wanted to scare them a bit so they hit the brake hard. The other driver drove right up beside us and started shouting and cursing. But my partner later said that in that moment, they regretted reacting like that in the first place, that they had their partner and friend in the car after all and should've been more considerate of them. The friend just exploded in anger. He rolled down the window and started going, 'You fucking son of a whore, you son of a bitch,' just going off like that. I was taken aback. The friend came to his senses and kept apologising to us and berating himself all the way home. Saying that he hated himself when he got like this.

But I was actually envious of him. If only I were a big, strong man, then I could do what he did . . . I wondered if he knew himself that he could do what he did because of how intimidating he looked. And because I used to be even more of an extreme personality in my early twenties, I hated being looked down on for being young so much that I would act like I was crazy to men. I did that at a bar once and a man hit me. My face was bruised and everything. I developed a phobia then and kept tamping down my emotions. And I imagined: if I had cursed like our friend from the passenger-side seat, would the other driver have come at me? Would he have really hurt me? Since there were more of us including a big man, wouldn't the other driver just curse a bit more and move on? I kept thinking things like that. I know these thoughts are wrong. But even so, I'd think, 'I can't do that, I'm not in the same position, men have more power,' which makes me want to do it too, to live like that as well . . .

Psychiatrist: Everyone has a moment where they want to be like that. When you're driving and someone makes you angry, you want to lash out, but there's that restraint that comes from rational thought. What if the other side had more people? What if they looked tough and had tattoos . . . Have you seen those sleeves you can put on that make you look like you have tattoos? (*Where did that come from?*) You make those calculations before you act, you see.

Me: Being around those men makes me really nervous, you know? And I feel so cowardly and stupid in my fright. Like, 'You can't even say anything because you're too scared anyway!'

Psychiatrist: Not at all. That's a very natural way to feel. Of course, everyone wants to be stronger or have more power, but that doesn't always manifest in violence. Maybe how you feel right now might spur you to some lawless prairie where you can walk around with a gun and shoot the bad guys (*I burst into laughter*). But you have rational thinking, so you step back. What happens if the other person presses charges? Or I get badly hurt? You think it through like that. I've seen so many people in my practice who are unable to restrain themselves and end up being violent. Especially those who have drinking problems. In a different scenario, let's say you saw your ideal type on the street. You might think, 'Wow, I want to hold their hand, I want to kiss them,' but you restrain yourself. It's all right to accept your natural urges instead of berating yourself for having them. And that's a healthier way to be, really. Because it's not like you're suppressing your anger or denying it, forcing yourself to see how beautiful the other person is.

Me: Right. I think I come down on myself too much for being scared of someone or for losing confidence in their presence.

Psychiatrist: But the thing about urges is that they're not always about fear. Sometimes, as I said about women earlier, an attraction or fascination towards strength can lead you to think more about women's rights or the disenfranchised, and your impulses and desire for compensation could be directed positively. It could end up becoming a motivating force in your life.

Me: You're right. I wish these impulses could lead to something healthier like that.

Psychiatrist: Your response was more than healthy. And the thing about dreams is that they allow your desires to let off steam for a bit. Bringing them into reality is a different proposition altogether, however.

Me: But isn't dreaming such dreams an indicator of a problem in your mental health?

Psychiatrist: On the contrary, it could indicate good mental health.

Me: Because I'm always thinking, 'My subconscious is such trash . . .'

Psychiatrist: Some things are better experienced through dreams than real life. Or if not dreams, then in writing. There are many alternatives. And I also hope you think of the fact that you didn't have extremely negative thoughts about the journalist when you were being interviewed as an indication of the expansion of your understanding of others, that you should think, 'Oh, I guess I can handle someone like that now.'

Me: Wow, it would be brilliant if I could – that's the right attitude. And that was why I didn't feel so bad during the actual interview, it was really in the conversation with my friend that everything fell apart. But the interview itself, it may actually have been a good thing. That I now have the strength to deal with that level of animosity, at least. Everything else that happened recently was fine, and I went out for a walk and took in the sunlight and had another conversation with myself, and that helped me regain my calm. I kept telling myself that there were lots of good things that happened in the past two weeks, why was I coming down on myself so much for that one incident, when I never bothered to praise myself when I did something right?

Psychiatrist: Excellent. And the thing about falling apart, look at it this way. Sure, you fell asleep in the middle of the day, but taking sleeping pills because you wanted to fall asleep and taking pills because you want to die are two very different things. In the past, this level of stress would've been enough to make you want to die, but now you think, I've come so far and done so much to be where I am now, am I really going to let this idiot topple me over? No way. And you decided to sleep it off instead. Think of it that way. You've grown.

Me: That's right. I wouldn't have wanted to die because of the journalist, I would've wanted to die because I hated myself so much, because I disgusted myself. I really would've wanted to die, too. But that wasn't my reaction, so I should feel like I'm getting better.

Psychiatrist: I'm glad. Because you really are.

I AM GETTING BETTER

'I can think, *I refuse to destroy myself because of something you did.*'

I had a hard week but I can feel myself getting better. I can control my feelings, and my recovery speed is also getting faster. I'm good at finding rational explanations. I still have points of vulnerability (dealing with hostile or condescending people who try to intimidate me) but compared to what I was like before, I go back to feeling like myself again much quicker.

Just the fact that a person like that can't kill me — in the past, I would've hated not just that person but myself for being victimised by that person and would have wished myself dead. My friend told me later she'd become afraid I would fall into self-hatred, that she was glad I came back from it almost right away.

I now know how to blame others for their wrongs. I can think, *I refuse to destroy myself because of something you did.* I'm more aware than ever that my life and my self are not so worthy of contempt. I know, now, that I must not try to overly censor myself, but to see myself from a generous and rational third-person perspective, to be observant and accurate.

I've improved a lot. I'm so glad that I don't need to repeat the same story over and over again like I did in book one.

9

IT'S NOT LIKE OTHER PEOPLE HAVE LIVED MY LIFE

I went to see an astrologer recently. I don't really believe in Saju fortune telling or Tarot cards, because I once went to a tarot café in Hongdae with a friend during the really dark time when I was working on my university transfer exam. The old woman who read my cards asked me about my current situation and declared, 'You will never get into the university of your choice.' How could she use the word 'never' so lightly? It was even more infuriating considering I ended up getting into the school I wanted.

But my friend had recommended this particular astrologer, so I had already gone once last year. They ended up getting some things wrong and some things right. The future hadn't happened yet, so I forgot about what they said about it. But that winter, I came across some transcriptions I had made of the session at the time, and looking back made me realise there were quite a lot of things the astrologer had gotten right. So I decided to pay them another visit, this time with my partner.

My reading came out more or less the same as the year before, while my partner was declared an extremely clever person who was a gifted speaker. My older sister had asked me to get her chart read as well, and she was judged as a femme fatale with a top-quality brain. I found myself asking the astrologer who was smarter, my partner or me. When the answer was my partner, I was annoyed.

I actually don't think I'm that clever, and I'm envious of people who are: quick on the uptake, finding the most optimal way of doing things. Despite my self-declared scepticism of astrology and tarot readings, I had ended up completely enraptured by what the astrologer was saying, and the thought that I was an easily influenced stooge – the only person in the world who didn't have firm roots – was painful.

Psychiatrist: How have you been?

Me: Not great.

Psychiatrist: Is there any particular reason?

Me: An incident. These days, I'm not as easily influenced by things as I was before, but I went to get an astrology chart reading yesterday. I'd done it last year and it was really accurate, you see. So yesterday I went with my partner.

Psychiatrist: How does that work?

Me: You give them your birth time, place and date. My previous chart reading had been so accurate that I began to blindly trust it. They do the chart on computers now. They told me about my partner's personality and characteristics and were totally accurate. My partner doesn't listen too much to others; they have the chart of a king, a leader. They hate losing, and once they begin something, they make sure they finish it. A really good personality. The fortune of a teacher and mine a student, apparently. I did agree with that a bit. My partner isn't forceful with me. I have a bit of hatred of men so I tend to take down them a lot, harass them and control them (*crazy*). I was like that to my partner in the beginning, but slowly I relented. I managed to reach a level of respect for them, and our relationship found its equilibrium.

And I keep becoming attracted to charismatic leader types, perhaps because I don't have those qualities. People who leave an impression, are overflowing with confidence, sure of themselves, eloquent. My older sister's chart says she's very clever. But I was told that in my chart, too. So I asked, 'Of the three of us, who is the smartest?' and the fortune teller said it was my older sister. 'What about me and my partner?' The answer was, '*Of course* it's your partner . . .' That was annoying. It hurt my pride.

Psychiatrist: It hurt your pride?

Me: Yes, my pride. Because it made me think of my brain as not being very good. It's a chip on my shoulder. My partner was just doing it for fun and didn't care one way or the other, whereas I was flipping out about the results. I told my friend who suggested the place that the fortune teller said I was the stupidest person, upon which the friend said, 'Well, you're not exactly the smartest person in the room all the time' and laughed. I was so annoyed about this I told my partner, who said, 'And is *she* some genius herself?' But I still felt bothered. So I tried another conversation with myself. I told myself that it was annoying but to not let other people make me think I wasn't smart. That the friend was the one who was being rude. This did make me feel a bit better about it, and it wasn't like I was in a position to yell, 'How much smarter are you to say that about me?' in that situation, so I hadn't said anything – but why didn't I let myself get mad, why did I think I wasn't smart? I'm wondering about that now.

Psychiatrist: What if the fortune teller had said you were the smartest?

Me: I would've felt good.

Psychiatrist: Just felt good? Would you have completely trusted this person saying that?

Me: What do you mean?

Psychiatrist: It's not like they administered an intelligence test on you. This judgement was made based on where you were born and when.

Me: That's true, but I was mad at my friend for saying that I wasn't the smartest person in the room all the time. I don't know why they think so little of me.

Psychiatrist: Do you think the astrologer's remark meant anything? They probably picked up on you being interested in who was smart or not, leading them to joke about the person sitting next to you being smarter.

Me: Wouldn't that be twisting things to make myself feel better?

Psychiatrist: For example – not that I think this incident is one that merits a discussion on credibility – let's say a set of triplets go see this fortune teller. They should have the same fortune and the same intelligence. Do they?

Me: But to say someone is smart and someone isn't, it's insulting.

Psychiatrist: But you asked them that.

Me: Only because they had said I was 'pretty smart' but raved about my sister and my partner being practically geniuses (*why be so overt about it*).

Psychiatrist: The standards for judging whether someone is smart or not are vague, anyway. You can say that a smart person is someone who has a high IQ or someone who is street-smart, quick on the uptake. But you went to that astrologer with a very trusting attitude, putting yourself in the weaker position to begin with. The astrologer probably thought they could say anything they wanted and you would believe them.

Me: Oh . . . my partner also teased me. That I had fanatic trust in this person, like they were the messiah. And because they didn't believe in any of that stuff at all, the astrologer seemed pitiful if anything. When the astrologer said my partner was smart and articulate and a teacher, they teasingly said, 'Well, it must be quite stressful for you to teach children who happen to be stupid or distracted,' but my partner doesn't think that way at all, not in the slightest. They said the astrologer seemed to have these ideas about people being fated to live the lives they were born into, whereas my partner believes everyone has their own process of changing who they are, and they pitied the astrologer because of it.

Psychiatrist: Do you think your partner was referring only to the astrologer?

Me: You mean, they were saying it to me as well?

Psychiatrist: A little bit? I think your partner meant you should just take this fortune-telling as something fun and nothing more. Because you know how fortune-telling is. Silly stuff about people being fated to live a certain way, that effort is meaningless.

Me: You do find it funny that I'm taking something like this so seriously, right?

Psychiatrist: It's all very well to feel good when you hear something you like, but I hope you only take it as one piece of advice among many others. Here's an example from my own life. I have this friend who loved getting her fortune told. She was really proud of her fortune. The thing about Saju fortune-telling is that the results will be the same whoever tells it, but she was very happy about the fact that every Saju fortune teller would say she had the best fate. I fell out of contact with her for a while, but once we reconnected, she told me about how her parents had lied to her about her birthdate all this time, that they had claimed she'd been born on a day that had an excellent Saju chart. She'd had her fortune told hundreds of times, but it had all been a lie. And no matter how famed a fortune-teller she went to, not once did any of them pick up on the fact that this was not her real birth-date. A case of suggestibility, if you will. Those with developed suggestibility tend to pay more attention to the parts they prioritise. But there are so many things you can solve with effort, correct? Just like when you have your conversations with yourself to assuage your hurt. I want you to prize that quality more from now on. More than where and when you were born.

Me: What about my obsessing over what my friend said?

Psychiatrist: Your friend's words might have a different meaning. Maybe they know you well and were teasing you.

Me: I took it as them thinking of me as stupid. That's how I felt. I fell into self-castigation for the first time in a long while. I just kept going back to it. That I'm weak at the foundation, I get influenced too easily by other people. I really hated myself, especially when I began feeling intimidated by my partner after the fortune telling. That I had dealt with them as my equal until now, when they were actually much stronger than I am, when I'm this weakling . . . that kind of influence.

Psychiatrist: You've given the fortune teller too much authority: the authority to judge. You should have the authority to judge for yourself, especially when you've spent more time with your partner than the fortune teller has. They would've made their judgement just by a birth-date, even if they'd never met your partner.

Me: Right? I've spent all this time with my partner, why am I swayed by this tiny piece of evidence? That made me really mad at myself. My partner didn't even care, why was I so obsessed . . .? It's so pathetic for someone who's almost never paid attention to astrology to be so obsessed now (*really pathetic*).

Psychiatrist: I hope you take a step back and think a bit more about the things you've managed to build through your own effort.

Me: I will. But I really want to become a stronger person. Which is why I keep wanting a Saju chart like my partner or my older sister. I want to be the king, the chief. Because I don't have those qualities. I'm always attracted to strong people because I'm not like them. I hate that I'm not like them, that I'm this weakling, and that's why I keep pretending I'm intimidating when I'm really not.

Psychiatrist: Everyone wants to be strong. It's very natural to have the desire to be sound and perfect when given a choice. But in becoming stronger, I think you should consider more scientific and rational methods. I want you to believe in your experience.

THE URGE TO PROVE MYSELF

'Who is the tiresome one here?'

There's a type of person who makes me feel small and shabby. They talk about themselves a lot, sucking all the air out of the room or making me feel hurt (I'm sure I've been guilty of this in the past myself, as much as I desperately hope it isn't the case). In the moment, it's just a brief spurt of annoyance but the real problem lies in how pathetic I feel afterwards. Why do I feel like that?

People like this seem to regard me like I'm a statue, an object, not a person like them, someone who is not as smart as they are. They themselves are the answer, the truth, whereas in comparison I am a flake, a piece of fluff, a non-starter. Is this merely self-pity?

In any case, I can't just listen to someone. I like talking about myself, and I tend to think I've no reason to spend time with anyone who doesn't ask me about myself. Anyone who just talks about themselves might as well just talk to a wall.

It exhausts me to meet people who go on and on as if they're trying to prove how much better they are than others. Their tiresome energy wears me out. I should not say anything, but when there's no one to impress but this one person, I try to get in as much about myself as possible as well, try to say more, to be more noticeable, even if it means making things up.

Who is the tiresome one here?

Me? Probably. I bet it's me.

Which is why I have to have a lie-down for the second day in a row.

I'm so tired of myself.

10

BEING MYSELF WHETHER IN HONESTY OR HYPOCRISY

Psychiatrist: How have you been?

Me: So-so. There was an interesting incident.

Psychiatrist: What happened?

Me: Not an incident really but a question. There's this author I like who's a bit older than me. We've known each other online for a long while and recently met in person for the first time. It was fun. But when I meet someone I'm not familiar with, I tend to be quite friendly. I smile, I'm polite, and go through the motions (*when I feel like it, at least*). And I was like that on that day. The author was also very polite. But not in an overdone way. It made me think a lot on my way home. Was my friendliness trained into me? Sure, I feel good after being friendly to other people, but sometimes I feel really tired after a day of doing that, especially when I didn't really want to, dammit. Not that I want to be rude, but I don't want to make a huge effort trying to keep the mood all light and happy, either. But I think it was because I acted that way that the people around me could tolerate me. There are lots of people who become shy in front of those they're not familiar with. I tend to set the tone in conversations with such people. But I don't want to do that. When I come back home, I'm all exhausted. Which is why it makes me wonder if my politeness was just trained into me. I want to not smile when I don't feel like smiling and not always be making an effort to get along.

Psychiatrist: You said you had this feeling on your way back from the meeting. Do you ever have the feeling when you're in the middle of being friendly?

Me: Yes. Sometimes. 'You know, I'm a little tired.' That kind of thing.

Psychiatrist: What about the other person?

Me: They don't seem to be putting in as much energy as I am. They're not rude, just not as effortful, like they're acting like they normally would (*this is just my own impression and not necessarily the truth*). Why am I putting in such an effort, then? Like that.

Psychiatrist: Did the author seem rude to you?

Me: Not at all. They struck me as a bit egocentric. They do what they want to do, which made me wonder if the people around them end up altering their own behaviour to accommodate them. Which made me feel a little, uh, disappointed? Because I'm always accommodating others. I like it when other people accommodate me, you see. The people in my life I am most comfortable with, namely my partner and family and close friends, accommodate me a lot. My attitude changes when I'm with someone new (*one of the things I hate most about myself*).

Psychiatrist: What do you think it does for you, for the people around you, to be so accommodating?

Me: I am always very honest with them. My family because they're my family . . . oh, with my friends? When we become close, they accommodate me more.

Psychiatrist: Everyone tries to be accommodating at first.

Me: Everyone?

Psychiatrist: You're saying you're accommodating at first and then not to the people you're close to. What's the process that enables this? I'm sure you don't wake up one day and say, 'I

won't be so accommodating to you anymore.'
(*I burst into laughter.*)

Me: Hmm . . . I think I slowly start to assert myself. Well. I don't know, actually.

Psychiatrist: Are there any people who grow distant because you assert yourself?

Me: To be perfectly honest, I have no friends I am truly myself with aside from the friend I mentioned who teased me about being stupid. I have very few friends. The ones I have now are really old ones . . . we automatically accommodated each other as time went on. Aside from that, there are zero friends I've had deep relationships with through this mutually accommodating process. I only accommodate my partners in the beginning. When we're getting to know each other.

Psychiatrist: Everyone at some point is someone you once were getting to know. I want you to think of your relationships as being the fruit of the effort you put into them.

Me: But why do I have to put effort into that? (*Surprised.*)

Psychiatrist: Because everyone does.

Me: Really?

Psychiatrist: Yes. Everyone has different levels of effort they put into a relationship. And the discrepancy this time may have come from a difference in your ages or social standing. But even in such situations where you feel like you're putting in more of an effort, part of living in the adult world is about hiding who you are for a bit and trying to accommodate the other. I hope you don't generalise your efforts to the point of unduly criticising yourself.

Me: You mean, I always act like the victim and the weak one? That I always have that tendency? Why am I like that? Because I have so little self-esteem, again?

Psychiatrist: Instead of looking for the reason for it, why not think of your friendliness and approachability as a strength?

Me: Some people say they're envious of me for being like that. My partner says they envy my empathy and how I can laugh and cry with other people. That they try to understand others but there's always a limit. But I think I let others too much into myself and I hate that.

Psychiatrist: You're right in that it can definitely get to be too much letting other people in. But that author who was perhaps a little cold if polite might be thinking, 'How lovely she is to someone she has only just met.' And relationships are not immutable. Just like you built your relationships with your partner or your old friends, you could make a lot of effort in the beginning but become more comfortable with asserting yourself the second time you meet and still more the third. It's important to remember you've had people like that and still do (*do I really have people in my life now who I can build that kind of relationship with?*). Obviously, if I feel uncertain in a relationship, I hide myself more, and it could be a blow to my self-esteem if I feel like I'm *too* accommodating. But I could think to myself, 'I may not have anyone in my life who can save me, but this person can't save me either, so I'll just go back to being how I was before I met them.'

Me: To shrug it off that lightly? I'll try. And there's one more thing (*it's just endless*). In high school I had low self-esteem and I was very self-deprecating to the point where my friends would say, 'There you go, cutting yourself down again.' People don't say that to me anymore, which means I'm getting better, right? I think once you're used to putting yourself down, you let others put you down as well. Because you become less sensitive to the putdowns. I had this friend I felt thought very little of me. I've told you this before, but there was a girl in my final year of high school who would see me eating chocolate and say, 'That's why you're getting fat.' Those little things left big wounds, I have so many memories like that. But I couldn't tell her that she was hurting me. My friends habitually told me how oversensitive I was. So I didn't say anything. And it got to the point where I thought, 'She's always putting me down, I'm just going to cut her off.' And in an extreme fashion, I never spoke to her again. She was actually a very close friend, right? I think she was very taken aback. And three weeks ago, she sent me a message through Instagram. Saying she had missed me, but she hadn't had the courage until now to reach out. It made me think a lot. I wrote her a long reply talking about all the things I had kept inside me for so long. 'I used to think you were putting me down . . .' I was scared that if I met her, I'd go back to being that nineteen-year-old, that she'd cut me down, and I'd be unable to say anything and just accommodate her. She replied to that, saying she really hadn't understood and thanking me for being so honest with her. I'm actually visiting her later today, at the store she runs. I'm a little scared.

Psychiatrist: That's actually amazing of you.

Me: What?

Psychiatrist: You're amazing. Because you very honestly expressed your thoughts.

Me: Is that a big deal?

Psychiatrist: Absolutely. You said all the things you hadn't said when you were afraid of seeming oversensitive. You need to do more of this. It's impossible to predict other people's reactions to the things you tell them. Some people may react positively, like this friend, and others might go, 'How tiresome this all is.' The more you try to predict other people's reactions, the more negatively you will imagine them to be. But in this case, you've essentially sent her a message saying, 'This is how I feel about it, and if you don't understand it's all right if you never contact me again, I don't want to be hurt more than I already am.' You had been unable to handle your hurt as a teenager, but as an adult you have proven you can process things responsibly. Because you can be more clear with others about your thoughts and feelings now.

Me: That's true. I was grateful to her for apologising, and it was a big relief to send off that reply. I cried a lot that day. Having resolved a buried hurt made me cry with relief and realise it was not such a big deal after all, and it made me stop resenting my friend. I'm worried about my ingrained friendliness now, so I'm wondering if I have to be cool about it, or just be the way I am . . .

Psychiatrist: Be the way you are. Because if you're in a position to talk about yourself now, you can bring forth the friendly memories and feelings, and overwrite your negative memories with new ones.

Me: All right. I'll have a good time with her.

AN INGRAINED POLITENESS

'I was truly afraid of being ostracised.'

I thought about why I am overly polite to people who are not important to me. It's because they can hate me at any time. Because they can judge me and resent me for the smallest things I do. Meanwhile, because the people who love me already love me, and there's a low chance they'll start to hate me, I get snappy with them.

What I realised this time around is that my politeness has been learned over a long period of time. I've been told to be polite since I was little and made to think it was my obligation to be obsequious to others. I didn't want to be hated, and I was truly afraid of being ostracised.

But on days I perform politeness for long stretches of time, I collapse into bed. The fatigue lingers. I can never leave behind the fear of someone hating or resenting me, and I probably never will. But I still want to be free. Even if I'm left behind by everyone, insulted by everyone, and end up completely alone, I want to throw aside this façade. I don't want to be polite or seem like a good person – I'm not a good person anyway. Replying politely to social media comments, the emails I send where I verge on fawning. Wearing a mask of politeness with others, reacting and smiling at the right things at the right time.

When it gets to be too much, I will stop. Anytime, when my heart is no longer in it. I need to be myself sometimes. I hate myself for realising this so late, at the age of thirty. This self-hate that's as serious as my self-pity, I have come to accept that it's a part of me as well.

11

DO I HAVE GUMPTION OR NOT?

I work out three times a week, but I entered a bad period where I was suddenly stressed about how I looked. I had visited my mother and grandmother and my mother said I was getting fat, that I needed to lose weight – I was furious. Why did she keep saying that to me? Mother said she was fine with how I looked but I seemed stressed, so wouldn't it be better if I lost the weight? 'Then why did you bring it up when I didn't say anything about it? Why are you trying to hurt me?' My grandmother hugged me as I cried. Older people have different standards of beauty, and my grandmother said I actually needed to gain weight, that I was too skinny. When my mother objected, my grandmother shouted at my mother telling her she was being ridiculous, that she would refuse to see me if I lost more weight. I cried again and said I wished everyone had my grandmother's standards. But because I happen to be a part of this era and not my grandmother's, I went to a three-week diet camp where they make you exercise constantly.

Psychiatrist: So how was that experience, did it live up to your expectations?

Me: My weight, you mean? Do I look thinner? Can you tell?

Psychiatrist: Well, you have finer features to begin with, and you're in winter clothes.

Me: Oh, I do? I lost about four kilos of body fat. Doctor, I was a whole fifty-seven kilos.

Psychiatrist: Is that a lot?

Me: It is. I'm only 161cm tall. I extended my stay by a week and stayed there for three weeks total.

Psychiatrist: Because it was effective?

Me: Because I liked it there. I'd been doing nothing these past few months, with no plans. I'm actually really good at sticking to plans, but I've had nothing like that in my life recently. I wanted to manage my time better, and it wasn't working for me. But at the camp I had a schedule from 8 a.m. to 7 p.m., which was very stabilising.

Psychiatrist: And the schedule was geared towards your health as well?

Me: Exactly, and wow, it was five, six hours a day of exercise. It was really hard. Hard but nice. The boredom was the hard part. The first week was torture, but the second week felt good. Which is why I extended my stay. I thought of doing maybe a full month, but went for just an extra week instead, at the end of which I thought, 'I should've signed up for a month.' It would've been cheaper to do so.

Anyway, on the fourteenth day, a Saturday, I went to a wedding and then came here just for my prescription and went home. I thought I'd be glad to be back, but I really hated it. I was afraid that I'd go back to the boring and hard times of before, that all the bad memories were coming back, even if it was a space I loved. You know how I love my dogs more than anything, but raising them is hard? Love and suffering are two sides of the same coin. Because I have three dogs, all of my free time is taken up with caring for them (*my family took care of my dogs during this period*). Thinking of how my freedom would be cut in half again when I returned to real life made me feel frustrated. I do miss my babies, but it's also freeing for me now. Something like the way mothers feel when they're temporarily relieved of their children: I'm free! But maybe these feelings were because I was a week away from my period.

Psychiatrist: Were you preparing yourself mentally for your return when you were leaving the house?

Me: Yes. And I wasn't in a good place around the second week. I kept crying. I was fine when exercising, but during the half-hour breaks I might feel really great and then be overwhelmed by feelings of emptiness. My period started on the third week, and I must've also gotten used to the activity, because I was fine. And I like being alone, so exercising and eating and resting in my room alone, all that was really great. I also befriended someone there who was twenty years old. A really nice person.

Psychiatrist: I'm glad you had a good time.

Me: Right? And something that was a bit sad was the fact that there weren't many people around my age up to their forties. People who were at the prime of their working lives, in other words. Everyone there was mostly college students or graduates or mothers who had children who were a bit older. I don't think it's really possible for someone with a day job to be there. The stress of work makes them eat, there's no time for exercise, and they still have to work – on repeat. I was like that. I felt really lucky I got to be there.

The camp was nice, and when I got back, I got a bit anxious and started making plans. I haven't stopped moving since Friday, signing myself up for personal training, going to the clinic. But I think I'm exhausted now. Two days ago, I was completely enervated. Not a single bit of strength left in me. So I cancelled everything.

Psychiatrist: It's a good thing you have lots to do, but I hope you've left room for relaxation every now and then.

Me: I'll do that. Also, I've started studying feminism again.

Psychiatrist: Why are you studying again?

Me: I didn't read while I was at camp. I was too focussed on exercise. But an author friend of mine I like is putting together a short film. I supported her and joined her crowdfunding. She started tweeting so I followed her. The world of Twitter is, to me, a little harsh and strong? That's the impression I get. Lots of extreme talk.

There was a (*highly retweeted*) tweet that sounded like me from before. You know how you're bound to make a mistake if you tend to act differently to most people? You're bound to slip up. This tweet was cutting someone down for a mistake they had made, as if they themselves could never possibly make such a mistake. For example, it's up to you as to whether you choose liberal feminism or radical feminism, but you shouldn't cut down and exclude whichever side you don't support. But I feel like there are many people who act like every issue could be as neatly sliced in half as a turnip.

Psychiatrist: An exclusionary attitude, a disrespect for the choices of others.

Me: Right. I know that having a cause and fighting for it is impressive. Very much. How could I criticise that? But the duelling of extremes is tiring, and I myself feel uncertain about the issue, which makes me read a lot. I want a solid point of view. The 'corset' controversy made me think, 'Why do I try to lose weight, why put on make-up, is it really to be loved by men? Is it display?' But it really isn't just that. I think the problem lies in the culture itself. The kind of culture that somehow makes us think men value power or money while women value looks – who came up with that in the first place? And the culture where everyone is assumed to be heterosexual. And I've felt that the skinny, pretty girls have always been acknowledged more, noticed more, and valued more, ever since I was little. Which makes me feel more competitive when I'm among women. And I hate that about myself.

Psychiatrist: You hate how you're like that?

Me: Yes, a lot. Even at the diet camp. A whole bunch of skinny women came in when I was about to leave. There were some very beautiful women. I felt so competitive all of a sudden. 'Am I prettier than her? Is she thinner than me?' I'd stare at them working out and feel so much hatred for myself. But who cares if someone is skinnier than I am, or heavier than I am? I hate myself for the reassurance I feel when I see someone heavier than me. And this looking at women's faces, trying to see if they are prettier than me or not. I normally never bother to look at other people in the first place, I just put on my glasses and do my own thing on the treadmill. Otherwise, I'm looking down at them, judging them as being less than me. So I began to think, why was I trying to compete with other women, was it all to impress men? I couldn't get to the bottom of it, and even if I were a victim of patriarchal conditioning, it's not such an easy thing to overcome, and it's hardly my fault – I'm just a single individual. Did that mean obedience to the status quo was my limit, did I have to 'throw off the corset' myself? I wasn't sure what would make me happy.

Doctor, I know this is extreme, but I need to tell you one more thing. It's important to me that I've lost enough weight so that when I sit down, my stomach folds less and I feel lighter. I want to keep exercising. Because I hate eating and drinking and being stressed and ruining my body. I want to be healthy and feel good.

And I want to look good and be happy with that, but once I've done the full setting (*make-up, hair, clothes all styled*), I become obsessed with how much prettier I look. When I'm not wearing make-up, I don't care what I look like when I go out because I know I'm ugly. I don't bother looking at other people and just walk around as I please. But when I'm all done up, I find myself staring at people prettier than I am, or slimmer. I compare myself to them. I'm not happy with that. Does it mean I'm probably better off nor wearing make-up and cutting my hair short?

Psychiatrist: Do you think that would be easier?

Me: Why am I tearing up? Doctor, I'm really confused. Do you know anyone else who talks about this stuff? (*Thinking about other people again.*)

Psychiatrist: (*Does not answer question.*) Everyone is different. Some don't care how they look to men, others take great care with their make-up and appearance.

Me: But women feel more pressure to look good. Like it's a necessity, not a choice.

Psychiatrist: It's not necessarily that women are pressured into it, but it's part of a competitive system.

Me: So why does that competitive system exist? (*I sound accusatory.*)

Psychiatrist: You can say it's an effect of the patriarchy, but women taking care of their looks has become socially acceptable. In the past, European men took exaggerated care of their looks, but now it's considered unattractive if a man cares too much about his appearance. Things change with time. You don't have to overthink it beyond that point. I don't think you need to put too much declarative emphasis on doing or not doing your make-up or cutting your hair or getting plastic surgery. Not long ago it was considered unacceptable to have short hair, now we take it for granted that we can have different hairstyles. Everything we do, now, seems to lead to issues of hate and discrimination.

Me: I think children are beginning to hate their own bodies. I was like that in high school, I'm sure it's much worse now. Even as a high school senior, the girls would say things to me if I showed up without make-up, and that made me think it was shameful to have a naked face. It took me a long time to leave the house without make-up. I hardly think I put on make-up because I want to?

Psychiatrist: That's if you were considering the time before you wore make-up, but, conversely, think of the first time you put it on. Don't you think that time, at least, you were doing it for your own satisfaction?

Me: Because I looked prettier with it on?

Psychiatrist: Yes. Surely there are parts of the issue that just happen to be so, but putting a label on every single thing, including these naturally occurring parts, would just be a never-ending endeavour, I think. Maybe all this studying to make your perspective more defined will lead to more discomfort. I'm just not sure if it will help you come to a neat conclusion. I think you'll end up even more confused.

Me: Then what should I do?

Psychiatrist: Do it only up to a degree. Don't lose yourself in it. There are things that are more important to you right now. Instead, you're primed to see everything you do as some kind of sin.

Me: You're right. Why am I so easily suggestible? Doctor, do I really not have a mind of my own? I asked my partner and they said I needed to be more grounded in myself. I don't know how.

Psychiatrist: I told you once that extremes tend to connect, right? I think your lack of affiliation makes you want to create one. Like declaring, 'I'm a feminist!' Why not lay off on the reading for a bit. It'll help ground you more.

Me: I don't know if it will. Anyway, what should I do about the medication?

Psychiatrist: I'm wondering if we should add the medication even though it made you a bit anxious last time.

Me: No.

Psychiatrist: I'll just put a little bit in. If you feel you're reacting to it, we can take it out.

Me: All right. What colour is it?

Psychiatrist: It's very tiny, mint-coloured. Just half a pill. I think we can start decreasing your medications a bit (*great news, for once*). You seem to be doing well.

Me: Really? I'm so glad. I really don't feel too bad. I'll try to get stronger in mind and body. I think my depression has really receded. I'll keep working out.

Psychiatrist: Great, have a good weekend.

I KEEP FORGETTING THE BASICS

'Nothing is absolute.'

I'm trying to become stronger in mind and body, but it's hard. Even when I'm not a direct victim and only a bystander, certain incidents make me very upset. I'm beginning to realise how monstrous my extreme thinking was, how I cut down myself and others, how I would cut people out of my life for any tiny mistake or flaw or misunderstanding. My rigid thinking made me and everyone around me suffer. I'm still like that to some degree but I'm getting better.

The kind of confidence that makes people mock others as if they had never made a mistake in their lives, that makes people act like their way is the only way – this kind of confidence fills me with dread.

Anyway, one must admit things quickly, reflect deeply but not for too long and commit to doing better immediately. Nothing is absolute. And I must not impose my thoughts on others. It's these basics that I unfortunately keep forgetting.

12

FLEXIBLE THINKING AND THE COURAGE TO REST

Me: Hello, doctor.

Psychiatrist: How was the extra pill this time around?

Me: It made me feel bad so I immediately took it out. The one day I took it, I had such terrible heart palpitations that I took it out the next day and I felt all right again. It was such a small dosage, but what a reaction! I don't think that pill is right for me. What is it?

Psychiatrist: It helps regulate dopamine and serotonin. The medication you're on now helps increase your dopamine and serotonin. It's a bit tricky to explain, but the extra pill can create a heightening effect. I've never seen anyone who reacts to it this way. It's good that you took it out. Have you been working out?

Me: Of course. Every single day.

Psychiatrist: Every single day since our last session is just three days. (*I'm dead.*)

Me: You're right.

Psychiatrist: Do you take Sundays off?

Me: Yes. The gym closes then. I had my first personal training session, and I thought I was going to die. It was the hardest exercise I had ever done in my life. They analysed my body for its weak spots and we began strengthening them. I'm very good at squats but my glutes and hamstrings are weak. Doing those workouts was extremely hard for me. My trainer kept saying I could do it, but I wanted to punch them. But my legs shook so much after that I did feel like I had a good workout. The moment where I just couldn't take it anymore, they let me off.

Psychiatrist: I hope your trainer is a good one. Any other incidents?

Me: Let's see. I thought a lot about what you said about me studying feminism, and it made me realise I had considered feminism as a kind of religion. I think it's fine in general if I have an ideology to follow and value. But I was like a Christian feeling sorry for atheists for not having a God, in some ways. I pitied those who didn't understand feminism, to the point of thinking my life would've been easier, too, if I didn't know about feminism (*such arrogance*). I realised such thinking was very dangerous. I still think feminism is very important. But I shouldn't force my thoughts on anyone, not that I went around proselytising. Everyone has their own multi-faceted life, and to pity someone while in ignorance of what their life is like is very arrogant and just wrong. A realisation that made me feel better about things.

You said to me last year that I seem like I would like an author, find one thing I don't like about their work and completely chuck them. I really was like that at one point. This incident made me realise once more how dangerous that kind of thinking is. To see someone in fragments and pieces and judge their whole being based on one small element. I do think I'm much better about it than before.

Psychiatrist: Are you still studying up?

Me: I haven't been reading as much since then. I felt the need to give it a bit of a rest.

Psychiatrist: I like that you haven't dumped it wholesale and are giving it a rest instead. In truth, it is very common to see one side of someone and judge their entire being for it. A generalisation. There's a famous person who comes to this clinic. Well, 'famous' isn't quite the word, they're someone who went viral on the internet for one thing. Basically, they were hounded for this one small thing, mocked by people who could never understand their whole being. They're a bit older, too. I'm guilty of that myself. If I see someone's writing on the internet, I might think, 'This person probably believes this and has these thoughts,' and until that person sits in front of me and tells me their story, I wouldn't have guessed their complexity (*but isn't that obvious?*).

Me: What do you mean, you wouldn't have thought they were the same person?

Psychiatrist: That this person in front of me would've been active on the internet.

Me: Oh, yes, that's not always obvious. Of course.

Psychiatrist: Anyway, it got resolved. But the internet doesn't allow for facial expressions, communication is always flawed and people don't want to hear the other side of an argument, which makes it impossible to see all the facets of a person. It makes you think of how dangerous such a situation could be.

Me: Yes. I realised I was like that. The one saving grace is that I had come to feminism after realising how I tended to generalise a whole person from just a single aspect of them, so I try not to judge people for thinking differently from me. I don't make other people uncomfortable because of my beliefs. I'm glad for that, at least.

Psychiatrist: Let's think it through from the beginning – why you got interested in feminism in the first place. I strongly think it was because of your general interest in the disenfranchised.

Me: I think you're right.

Psychiatrist: Everyone needs to pay attention to the disenfranchised, and it's good to be attentive to those around us, but I think you should also spend a little more time looking into your personal points of vulnerability or thinking of things you can enjoy.

Me: Yes, which is why I'm working out and looking into taking music lessons so I can write songs as a hobby. There's a music hagwon right next to the gym. I'm thinking of starting next week. Doesn't that sound neat?

Psychiatrist: Yes, and I've always heard that going to those hagwons makes you a much better singer.

Me: I hope so. And that diet camp you didn't want me to go to at first, I'm really glad I went. I know you didn't want me to quit my job, either, but quitting was one of the best things I did. You say I'm too easily influenced sometimes, but I think I'm getting good at making the final choice on my own.

Psychiatrist: You're right.

Me: The best thing about having gone to diet camp is that I'm a lot more proactive about things, I think? And I had a thought: I hope if I ever come to a point where I'm doing nothing, it won't be because I couldn't be bothered with anything. I mean, I want to have a better reason than just not wanting to be bothered. So I've been doing everything I've put off, and it's made me a little busy. Nothing much, just bank errands and things like that.

Psychiatrist: To make a habit of continuing things and getting things done is in itself an excellent development. When one thinks, 'I am depressed,' it makes them stay at home more and be helpless and meet fewer people and get cut off from society. In such cases, it is the habits we developed when we were not depressed that help us slough off that depression. One might say they're doing a certain thing because they're depressed, but such behaviour may be exacerbated by a habit of withdrawing from society. If we make a habit of doing a certain thing when our serotonin levels are high (*when our condition is good*), the possibility of creating more good days by trying to be the selves we were at that optimal state would be that much greater.

Me: That's very true. And I don't even have time to be depressed these days. A lot of my depression has been mitigated. My mood is still hard to control sometimes, it goes up and down. And I'm very sensitive. But a lot of my depressive and helpless moments have disappeared because I no longer automatically stay in bed just because I happen to tell myself, 'I'm depressed, I'm helpless.' And letting go of the pressure of filling my days with activity has let me relax more. But I'm so busy. Working out takes out three hours of my day, and my diet lets me eat 1,000 to 1,200 calories a day, and the lack of carbs makes me feel tired.

Psychiatrist: Sunday is your cheat day, then.

Me: It is. I ate a normal meal on Sunday and I felt much stronger.

Psychiatrist: It's good to set small goals and reward yourself when you meet them.

Me: Since diet camp I've only lost 0.1 kilograms, now that I'm not doing the really strict on-site regimen. I wanted to compensate for that. But you know how your body changes if you've been exercising for a while? My body looks different than before. Jeans that didn't fit me before now fit. Oh, and I wanted to tell you something, I want to become vegetarian.

Psychiatrist: (*Bursts into laughter.*) Why is that?

Me: So random, right? I've been thinking about it for a while. Because you can always ignore things, just turn away. You can always decide to live whatever life is most comfortable for you. But I have dogs. The argument goes, why are pets not all right to eat, but cows and pigs are fair game? And they have a point. I want to say that it's not eating animals that's the problem, it's factory farming. Is it ethical to eat cows and pigs when you know about factory farming? And I looked up videos about it, which were truly horrible. Why are you smiling?

Psychiatrist: Well, a video can be edited to present the perspective of whoever is producing the video.

Me: I know all that, but factory farming is a reality, it's the truth. I read what pro-meat people wrote as well. Because it's important to hear what the other side has to say. But it made me think. I'm not saying eating meat is an absolute evil, or being vegetarian is an absolute good. But it's true that horrible things have been happening since the advent of factory farming and industrialised slaughterhouses. There are numbers printed on eggs. If the numbers have 1 at the end, it means the chickens could roam. If the numbers end in 4, it means the chickens were caged, laid by fowl that never had a chance to live out in open air.

I'm also curious about how exactly the animals that are given the animal welfare certification have their suffering minimised. Would that meat be good for my body in the end? The thought made me not want to eat it. And the thought of my choice to eat meat bringing terrible suffering to another living creature made a chill run down my spine. Why was I always going on about the disenfranchised but eating meat? So I decided to take on the vegetarian challenge.

Psychiatrist: All right. That's your choice. But I hope you're not too radical about it. What about taking gradual steps?

Me: All right. I really don't think I can touch meat for a while, but I'll do that. Why did you laugh when I talked about vegetarianism just now? That didn't make me feel good.

Psychiatrist: It's just that the conversation swerved in a random direction. It didn't feel like you went through a process there, just a sudden conclusion you came to with no warning.

Me: Oh, I see. You know, I wish there was a user's manual for my life.

Psychiatrist: Oh, I wish there wasn't.

Me: You don't? For me, you mean?

Psychiatrist: Yes.

Me: I don't know why I'm reflecting on my life all the time. I feel like I'm so inadequate, someone who has to fix things every day. My partner isn't like that.

Psychiatrist: But it means you're becoming a better person every day.

Me: Does it? My partner doesn't reflect on things. And sometimes, I think my partner is only wrapped up in themselves.

Psychiatrist: (...) Well, you are also influencing this partner who is wrapped up in themselves.

Me: I do think I am influenced more than I influence.

Psychiatrist: It's all a give and take. And you can discover things about yourself from people who are wrapped up in themselves. In any case, don't try to give yourself too much work to do.

Me: All right. I'm getting better, aren't I?

Psychiatrist: I think you're doing fine.

Me: I think so, too. But I keep thinking I'm so stupid.

Psychiatrist: See? Even if I tell you you're fine, you won't accept it. (*They know me too well.*) Like with any other thought, I hope you don't try to get to the bottom of this one too hastily. Like ending something with, 'I'm stupid!' and being done with it.

Me: All right. I'll remember. Oh, and another improvement is that I used to find myself thinking, 'I really like myself today', but now I find myself thinking, 'I don't think I like myself today.' Which means, I now normally like myself, and the times I don't like myself are the exception! I think this is progress.

Psychiatrist: Of course.

FINDING THE MANUAL THAT'S RIGHT FOR MY LIFE

'I'm trying to let go of my habit of generalising, of judging the whole by a little part.'

Just as I've said to the doctor, I used to have moments where I thought, 'I really like myself today', whereas now I have moments where I think, 'I don't think I like myself today.' My dominant mode of thought has changed. Also, I move my body a lot more. The diet camp really has made me less lethargic, or perhaps I became fed up with having lethargy be the reason behind my behaviour, so I've been taking care of the tasks I'd previously been neglecting. This has decreased the opportunities to be depressed. I don't have nightmares, and sometimes I talk in my sleep, but I don't really remember my dreams. I might find myself worrying, but if it's too much, I don't dig into it. I simply stop. My thinking has become more flexible. I'm trying to let go of my habit of generalising, of judging the whole by a little part. But I'm still wary of being easily influenced. Extreme emotions connect, they say. When I encounter something that moves me, I don't approach it rationally but emotionally, with fanatic attraction. This makes the people closest to me anxious, and while my depression is kept at bay, my mood keeps swinging and I become extremely sensitive and cry myself a river, and then have a lie-down, and then start the cycle all over again. A cycle that makes me think how hard it is to just live a life. I don't want to rush up the stairs only to tire myself out in the middle and roll back down to the bottom. I want to keep learning about myself and finding the best user manual for my life.

13

TO SEE THE PARTS OF MYSELF THAT SHINE

Me: Hello, doctor.

Psychiatrist: How have you been?

Me: I don't have a lot to report, to be honest.

Psychiatrist: That's good to hear.

Me: Right? The reasons behind my depression are clear now. I don't think I have any depressive episodes without cause. I'm feeling a little down right now, and you're always telling me to be specific with my feelings, so I tried earlier. I've kept my promise to exercise at least three times a week. But I haven't been watching my diet properly. I keep feeling hungry. So I felt my current gloom came from the endless hunger and the stress from my upcoming deadline. I also sleep a lot these days, and I haven't been getting good quality sleep. I keep talking in my sleep and waking myself from it. I recorded it. It sounds like I'm advising a friend: half of it is comprehensible and half is nonsense. I speak very naturally. When I wake, I don't remember what I was saying. I also nap a lot during the day.

Psychiatrist: Recent research on appetite says sleeping a lot could lead to heightened appetite.

Me: Sleeping a lot? But they say if you don't sleep a lot, you gain weight.

Psychiatrist: I mean in terms of quality of sleep. Increased REM sleep can break the balance of hormones that suppress appetite and make you more hungry. Also, you're in a situation where satisfaction can be elusive. You're not allowed to eat certain things, you have to meet your deadline. There are more things that stress you out than give you joy. You're feeling hunger emotionally, which naturally makes you think, 'Maybe my mouth could feel some joy at least.'

Me: Oh, I see. The jeans that fit me are starting to feel tight.

Psychiatrist: Already? It's only been a few days. (*This hurt.*)

Me: Yes, when I eat a lot. And I feel hungry no matter how much I eat, really, which stresses me out. Anyway, these are the reasons behind my melancholy feelings today. I get it. When it was possible to lose weight, exercise and maintain my diet without pain, I wasn't depressed.

Psychiatrist: Your goal then was dieting. You even went to diet camp for it. But you can't live like that now. I think it'll be better to think in the long-term instead of concluding that food is the reason for your feelings. I think we should control your sleep a bit with medication, since you're having conversations out loud.

Me: All right. And since I have so little to report right now, I've had to really think about what to say, and I had this thought. There was an acquaintance who revealed their dark past to me recently. I can't tell you what it is, but from my perspective, it is something major. I know such things happen often, and there are others who've experienced it, but listening to it made me feel really bad. I know I don't need to know the reason behind every problem, but I could understand why this person continues to suffer psychologically from what happened. But I don't have a terrible past like that. Sure, we were poor and there was domestic abuse, and my older sister was emotionally abusive and we had a codependent relationship, but my family and I have talked through it somewhat and we're doing better. But it made me think, why am I so depressed when I don't have a dramatic past like that? Why am I depressed at all? I know you must be tired of me saying the same thing over and over again, but I don't know why my depression and trauma persist for so long when nothing so serious has happened to me.

Psychiatrist: If you keep trying to find the reason behind your depression, you're going to look for some extreme reason or incident. And if you've experienced a terrible incident, it will obviously be that much harder to become healthy again. Yes, there are people who courageously overcome their pasts. Your own experiences, while not so dramatic when we think about them now, would've been extremely threatening to you back then. I'm sure you had all sorts of fears as a child when you saw your father hit your mother. The learned helplessness and the pressure to suppress your feelings in order to not set off anyone in your family (*my father, mother, or older sister*) would've transformed those suppressed emotions into a depression that dragged you down.

Me: And that's why I'm so sensitive to others' reactions?

Psychiatrist: It could be. There was also your older sister.

Me: Isn't it also a bit of an obsession, my trying to find a reason for everything? I mean, there's no real reason for hunger. I wonder if I should similarly accept depression as itself. And people do think of depression that way, but listening to my acquaintance made me think, 'Why am I so depressed?' And I also wonder why I'm especially sensitive to sexual violence in families.

Psychiatrist: The shock each person experiences in the face of a traumatic event is going to be different. Just as an event we consider shocking would be passed over as no big deal in another society. It all depends on the cultural environment and mood, or how easy or hard it is to come to an agreement on the extraordinariness of a situation. I wouldn't say you're oversensitive. I'd say it's your general regard for the powerless. You feel the same emotions towards victimised women as you do to your dogs.

Me: You're right. I read something fascinating in a book recently. It's from this book titled *Conquering Shame and Codependency* by Darlene Lancer where she explains that people who don't try to gain something from outside of themselves are those who end up gaining the most, that self-esteem and pride come from letting go of external validation. It made me think about how I'm always trying to gain something from the outside. I've always craved external validation, whether it was through knowledge or affection or esteem. But it's this very craving that indicates how I'm not enough to myself. I keep wanting to fix myself, to gain something better. It's exhausting. Wouldn't it be better for me to accept my flaws as they are?

Psychiatrist: Don't look at yourself in a negative way. You're trying to create some kind of ideal self (*a perfect me*) within you and constantly trying to live up to it. There's an obsession with forcing yourself into this ideal. Don't think of yourself as inadequate. You need to appreciate your positive qualities more than your negative ones.

Me: Oh, I see. You're saying I set these standards for what a person with high self-esteem should be, and try to force myself to meet these standards? In an extreme way?

Psychiatrist: You have strong tendencies towards doing that.

Me: I understand what you mean. But I think I can also consider my positive qualities as well. Sure, I still look more deeply at my negative ones, but it wasn't long ago that

I was completely blind to the positives, my gaze wouldn't even reach them. Now I do notice them on occasion. I notice them and appreciate them.

Psychiatrist: You do, it seems like it.

Me: I'm getting better, right?

Psychiatrist: You do seem like you're better. Later on, you'll be able to turn your gaze from a negative quality you've discovered to a positive one and think, 'I still have other qualities,' and not let it affect you so much.

Me: (*Moved.*) Thank you. Just to tell you one more thing (*so many things for a session where I said I had nothing to say*), I feel really pressured to not become egotistical or full of myself. I used to be bullied for being egotistical when I was in school. This was when I'd somehow become the queen bee of my group and it got to my head. A temporary insanity. The memories from that time are painful, but I'm also kind of glad about what happened to me. It made me come to my senses early, at least? I try not to be egotistical now. I'm also deathly afraid of the people I love leaving me if I ever change and become egotistical.

This has made me modest, but maybe a little too modest, I think. I keep telling my friends,

'If my book becomes a bestseller and it seems like I've changed because of it, you *have* to tell me.' My partner and I happened to attend one of my events together and I reiterated this sentiment to them again afterwards. They said, 'Actually, you have changed in a way!' I had been mad at the event planners for not letting me know the event's schedule and time until the day of the event, even when I called them directly. But even if I hadn't been the author, even if I'd been a publishing house employee, it's something that would've made anyone mad? And I'd been frustrated about it in front of my partner, and my partner said it was like I was saying, 'How dare they treat me this way!'

Psychiatrist: When that wasn't your feeling at all?

Me: It wasn't. I was shocked. I cried a lot and kept trying to explain myself. That I hadn't changed. My partner said they knew I hadn't changed; it had just felt like that in the moment. That they'd told me this story because I'd asked for an example. After I managed to stop crying and calmed down, I thought about it a bit more. Sure, my frustration could've been reasonably interpreted by my partner in that way. But the real truth of it was that when I'd asked the question 'Do you think I've changed?' I'd wanted their answer to be 'No.' And that had been a shock to me. After about an hour, I said to my partner that I probably secretly had not wanted to hear that answer. What I should've done was think to myself, '*Have* I changed?' and looked back on myself a little and fixed what needed to be fixed. There was no need for someone else's answer to have come as such a huge shock. I thought, 'Of course I could have changed, and if someone points that out, just fix your behaviour!'

Psychiatrist: Wouldn't not changing be stranger in this case? Regardless of how your book does, your talking about the ways in which you've changed through therapy *is* a change, albeit a good one. And you were invited to that event precisely because of your new fame as a writer. What I'm saying is, you could've let your frustration out over anything at all, and people would've thought, 'She's like that because she's a famous writer.'

Me: That's right. So I told my partner that if I'd still been a publishing house employee, my frustration would've been considered normal as well – but just because I'm a published writer now, weren't people interpreting my behaviour differently? It does make me a bit worried, that I could be acting the way

I usually do and others would be like, 'She's changed, she's become arrogant.' But didn't I handle this specific incident well enough?

Psychiatrist: You did. And I like what you said before, about admitting you've changed if you have, and if there's something you don't like about yourself, you can just fix it.

Me: Exactly. If I'd heard any of this before, I would've felt like my whole identity was being cut down. I would've thought I was completely ruined and irredeemable. 'I've changed into this person, I can never go back, I'll be ostracised.' That kind of thinking.

Psychiatrist: Anything about yourself that changes for the worse, you can always change back. And change isn't always negative, of course. You did well.

Me: Yes. I feel good, I feel like I keep getting better.

TO AFFIRM MY CHANGING SELF

'I'd confined myself to the wastelands within me.'

I don't want to be egotistical because I went through an egotistical phase, and I know what that was like. I want to be humble and empathetic. Even if I haven't been born with the kindest of hearts, I can at least try to experience and learn and change myself accordingly as I grow.

I know how to handle feelings of emptiness because I've felt empty. I am depressed, which is why I can find ways to not be depressed. But there was a time when I was determined such feelings of emptiness must never happen to me again, that if they did, I would take my meds and read and cry and stare down at the ground from the rooftop and feel the need to self-harm or even commit self-harm.

But instead of simply accepting how flawed I am, I've decided not to look at myself so negatively. There are lots of shiny and sparkly aspects of myself, too. I've just been trying so hard to not look at them. I'd confined myself to the wastelands within me, but there are geographies rich with green and blue inside me as well, which I will now try to spend more time in. I believe that I can do that now. That all of this is part of my own special effort to live on – the important thing, now, is to have faith in that.

14

BECAUSE LIFE GOES ON

It's not that my head is usually empty, but it's not as if I'm having profound thoughts all the time, either. Some days pass without epiphanies or special meaning, without extreme emotional highs and lows or particular incident. Some days are passed in boredom, others in contentment.

I wonder, sometimes, what it would be like if the rest of my days were like this. I would age, and repeating the same day over and over again would make my thoughts stagnate, with giant walls forming all around me. I would talk only to the person who remains next to me to the end and be isolated from the countless people in the world, only brushing past them. I may claim to hate such a life, but here I am without any plans, curiosity or motivation to do otherwise. A person who doesn't want to do anything. A person of congenital boredom and lack of fun.

Entering a new space can in itself be a huge challenge, and meeting new people might become much more difficult in the future than it is now. I am trying to think about what kind of life I want to live and what kind of person I want to become – and how far I am from being that. The distance to go is great, and my motivation not very. Sceptical as to whether curiosity can spontaneously arise, I continue to take my pills and go to therapy.

Me: Hello.

Psychiatrist: Hello. Did you get new tattoos?

Me: I did, these three. Cute, right?

Psychiatrist: Very. Was the pain bearable?

Me: The first two didn't hurt much. You know how the tattoo of Juding (*one of my dogs*) that I got on my arm was in the middle of my forearm? This time it's Suji and Boogie, which means my tattoos go all the way to the inner forearm now, which really hurt. The pain really is different according to the body part being worked on. My hands were shaking.

Psychiatrist: No regrets?

Me: None. I really like these tattoos.

Psychiatrist: (*Looks at them.*) This one says 'Hunger.'

Me: Yes. It's the title of a favourite book. I used the exact font they use on the cover.

Psychiatrist: How pretty. So how have you been?

Me: I only worked out twice this week. But I'm going today, so I'm keeping my promise to myself to work out three times a week. I ate a bit much this week and checked my body fat at the gym. My muscle mass has decreased a bit but, thankfully, no increase to my body fat. This week has been good in terms of getting work done. I made my deadline for my column, and my second book is coming together on schedule.

Psychiatrist: You've done a lot this week.

Me: Yes. I've been busy. Getting tattoos was also a big task, I actually had to make the time and physically go somewhere. And I didn't binge at home or anything when I needed to eat. I went to Seoul and had proper meals. I really like gnocchi. It tends to be a bit pricey, but I never regret paying for good food at a good restaurant.

Psychiatrist: Do you keep a food journal? (*I feel like it's turning more and more into diet therapy.*)

Me: I do. I ate a bit this week.

Psychiatrist: You should keep separate records of planned meals and unplanned, spontaneous eating. Sometimes, our emotional hunger makes us grab something to eat. I advise you to differentiate between emotional and physical hunger in your journal.

Me: Oh, I will. My emotional hunger moments this week were Sunday and Monday, which made it better. It was a bit intense on Monday.

Psychiatrist: Why on Monday?

Me: I was so hungry when I woke up on Monday. Normally, I don't feel that hungry. I'd eaten a lot on Sunday and was planning to not eat as much the next day, which stressed me out and made me want to eat more, I think. And for some reason, my condition was really bad. I couldn't get out of bed. I cancelled my personal training session and didn't go to the clinic.

Psychiatrist: When did you start feeling better?

Me: Around nine at night.

Psychiatrist: That's quite a long period. Even if you'd cancelled your schedule, I imagine you might have thought, 'I should still get up, I need to work out, walk the dogs,' and so on. Did you just feel like you didn't want to do all of that?

Me: You once told me to think, 'Just sleep', so I tried to do that, but I couldn't. Still, I kept busy this week. I kept going to places. So much so that I didn't have time to read.

Psychiatrist: Not even having time to read? That's new for you.

Me: I'm finishing up the transcripts for the second book. Once that's done, I'll show it to you, but there's a lot of it.

Psychiatrist: Isn't it painful to listen to your own recordings? As if you're experiencing those emotions again?

Me: Not really. It feels like I'm listening to someone else. I felt so much pain when I was transcribing and writing the first book. I felt self-pity. I cried. But the transcription process for the second book made me think, 'What a tiresome person. How tedious she is.' I could keep her at a distance, which was good. I also thought this time, unlike the first book, I wanted a proper conclusion. But I can't go, 'I'm cured now!' just because I've come to the end of the book. Not that I'm cured, either.

Psychiatrist: True.

Me: So I thought about the ways in which I've improved. I'm much less depressed, I'm very rarely found lying in my bed, and I no longer think, 'This was a good day', but instead think, 'This was not a good day' because my definition of a normal day has flipped from bad to good. And I move my body a lot more. I wasn't great with sleep before, but now I fall asleep easily when I feel sleepy, and when I begin to worry about something, I stop myself from spiralling because it's too much. I think it's a self-protective measure.

And my thinking is more flexible than before. I'm trying to correct my habit of judging a whole by its part, and I'm getting better at it. My suicidal ideations have lessened and so has my drinking. But I still have frequent mood swings, and the oversensitivity is still present.

Psychiatrist: Overall, excellent.

Me: I really don't have much to discuss with you anymore. I'll keep coming for treatment, my prescriptions will decrease as I get better, and I might get to a point where I can control my emotions without help, right? My resilience is much improved and I'm less influenced by things. Life goes on. I don't change dramatically, I might change a little and then go back to being the way I was, and these thoughts (*sudden tears*) make me think that the most important thing is to accept that this is life.

Psychiatrist: Past you is you, and current you is you as well.

Me: They're all me.

Psychiatrist: Yes. To say past you was incorrect and the current you is correct is also a bit odd.

Me: I don't think I was incorrect; I was sick. I can differentiate between sick me and healthy me.

Psychiatrist: But it could be something like this: some people feel great pain from just one tattoo, and there are those who get them all over their bodies but don't feel a thing. Like you said, it could be a question of which body part. Before, one part of your body could get hit and the whole body would hurt, making you think, 'My whole body hurts, I am truly weak.' And when another body part gets hit, you may not feel the same thing. You could've simply been hit on a weak part that first time.

Me: So my other parts may be strong, but I only happen to have been hit in a weak part?

Psychiatrist: Yes. Simply realising, 'It hurt when I got hit here, but I have healthy parts of me, too' is incredibly meaningful. Because once you know where you are weak, you can protect that part better.

Me: Then I want to find which parts of me are strong. Where are my strong parts? Because I'm always obsessed with what parts of me are weak. I'm envious of people who can immerse themselves in things they enjoy, people who can put their whole heart and soul into it. I have things I enjoy, too, but I don't think I put my everything into them. It may be a matter of never having discovered them. That's sad to me. I envy those who keep on doing the things they love to do no matter what anyone else says, no matter how useless that thing might be. I need to concentrate on that attitude of 'Well, *I* like it!' Like how I love ugly sweaters. They're so ugly and corny, and the patterns are so over the top, at times I've been reluctant to buy them, but I bought this one recently (*I am wearing a Christmas jumper*).

Psychiatrist: It's not ugly at all, it's pretty.

Me: I'm going to wear it all the time until Christmas. Because I can't wear it beyond then.

Psychiatrist: I've been thinking how pretty the colours are since you came in.

Me: Really? Thank you. And this is embarrassing, because I keep sounding like I'm about to reach enlightenment, but you know how life is just different for everyone? You can just live without liking anything much in particular. You can just live. Just like things a little, get tired of them, get passionate about them and then burn through them, or keep going with your lukewarm feelings about them, different people have different sorts of feelings. But even if I want to live like a passionate person, it does occur to me: 'Is there a reason I should criticise myself for not being such a person?

Wouldn't it be fine if I continued to live this way?' I might be a little obsessed with books, to be honest. But I don't want to tell people I love books because I think people consider it a little pretentious. When they ask, 'What's your hobby?' and I answer, 'Books,' they go, 'Hey, you're not in a job interview.'

Psychiatrist: (*Laughs.*) That's true.

Me: Lastly, I don't want to put myself down. Would it help if I stopped being self-deprecating?

Psychiatrist: Yes. There are many instances in which the words you speak affect your being. Your words are absorbed into you. For example, instead of saying 'It's the worst,' you can be a bit more specific, without going into the who, what, when, where, why, per se. Try using richer adjectives than good, bad or worst. Then you can be more specific with your emotions. You will be able to understand yourself better.

Me: And the emptiness? Is there something that can be done? Do you feel it sometimes, doctor?

Psychiatrist: Of course I feel lonely from time to time.

Me: Is it a matter of how much you feel it, then?

Psychiatrist: These are natural emotions. We reach out to people and build relationships precisely because we feel loneliness and emptiness. You can create some kind of routine to decrease your loneliness. It's an emotion we all feel, but because emptiness has been a part of your life for so long, you've fallen into this rut of thinking, 'I'm feeling this again, I feel like this every day, I'm just a lonely person forever.' But this is a necessary emotion. You need it to create relationships with others.

Me: I have to feel emptiness and loneliness in order to build relationships with others? That's a good thought. If I were fine alone, I wouldn't have to deal with anyone, right? I wouldn't have to meet anyone, either.

Psychiatrist: They are natural emotions that you are simply imbuing with a negativity that isn't inherent.

Me: I'm not like that. Sometimes, I enjoy the great emptiness I feel inside me. I kind of accept it. It's when these feelings continue for more than half a day that it gets hard.

Psychiatrist: To not let them persist for more than half a day is also an ongoing issue you will have to contend with.

Me: I don't need to fill my mind all the time, but I must think about what I want to fill it with when I do want to fill it. I'll get back to you on that.

JUST AS I LIVE WITH MY SCARS

'I have realised that there are feelings of emptiness that no one can fill.'

Antidepressants are used for depressions that go on for weeks, and because of them my rages and joys are short and shallow. These days, I don't fly into a rage or jump for joy. But just because my depression has lessened, it doesn't mean my personality has altered. It doesn't mean I've become happy, either, even if 'becoming happy' is in itself a contradiction.

Throughout my day I deal with boredom, helplessness and emptiness. My doctor says emptiness is a natural feeling, and now I understand what they mean. If this emotion is a lack, then I want to fill that lack, whether with my own thoughts or with other people.

I have realised that there are feelings of emptiness that no one can fill. I don't need to fill them, they cannot be filled and they are natural emotions that everyone feels. I have to embrace them, just as I have learned to live with my scars. Would a warmer embrace of other, more positive emotions be easier then?

Can the world be more beautiful and pleasant? I have such moments now, but can they take up more space in my future? That's how it must be for bright and lovely and energetic people. I don't want things to continue like they are now, where I'm neither depressed nor happy, living one day at a time without having anything I particularly want to do.

AFTERWORD

I NO LONGER HATE MYSELF

There was a time when I hated being seen so much that I would cover myself with my blanket, even when I was alone. When I felt the urge to cover myself in tattoos, when I only felt comfortable sitting in a dark room where I wore large sunglasses that covered half my face. A time when I desperately hoped I could be anybody else but myself.

The biggest gain from my treatment and publishing my book has been the fact that I no longer hate myself. I continue to accept the little bits and fragments of myself that my eyes and mind perceive and try to stop the horrible things that I would once say to myself.

I've come this far in my writing in the belief that what may be a tedious tale to some will be a story of hope for others. I am grateful to those who have read this account of an unexceptional person because our dark stories are similar, or maybe my story is completely unlike yours and yet you gave me your care. Lastly, I am thankful to my doctor and the precious people in my life who have enabled me to be myself.

I hope for the day when those who are unwell in the heart can get medical help as a matter of course and not be stigmatised for it or have their problems reduced by the people around them to evidence of weak will. When the wounds of the mind and soul shall carry the same weight of seriousness as the wounds of the body.

A NOTE ON THE AUTHOR

Baek Sehee studied creative writing at university before working for five years in publishing. For ten years, she received psychiatric treatment for dysthymia, which became the subject of her essays, and then her debut, *I Want to Die but I Want to Eat Tteokbokki*. Her favorite food is tteokbokki, and she lives with her rescue dog, Jaram.

A NOTE ON THE TRANSLATOR

Anton Hur was born in Stockholm, Sweden. He is the author of *Toward Eternity* and his translations include Bora Chung's *Cursed Bunny*, which was shortlisted for the International Booker Prize. He also enjoys tteokbokki.

A NOTE ON THE TYPE

The text of this book is set in Linotype Sabon, a typeface named after the type founder, Jacques Sabon. It was designed by Jan Tschichold and jointly developed by Linotype, Monotype and Stempel in response to a need for a typeface to be available in identical form for mechanical hot metal composition and hand composition using foundry type.

Tschichold based his design for Sabon roman on a font engraved by Garamond, and Sabon italic on a font by Granjon. It was first used in 1966 and has proved an enduring modern classic.